ROCK YOUR ROOKIE YEAR IN REAL ESTATE

Ramping Up Your Real Estate Career: Pre-Exam to Closing Your First Sale

Susan K. Gillis, M.A., Realtor®

ROCK YOUR ROOKIE YEAR IN REAL ESTATE By Susan K. Gillis, M.A.
RAMPING UP YOUR REAL ESTATE CAREER: PREEXAM to CLOSING
YOUR FIRST SALE

FROG POND PUBLISHING: www.FrogPondPublishing.com

Bulk ordering information: Special discounts are available on quantity purchases by corporations, educational institutions, associations and others. For details email the author or publisher email.

ISBN: 978-1-68-673865-4

First Edition

DEDICATION

This book is dedicated to those who truly want to make a positive impact; within themselves, for their families and the communities they serve. Your fortitude and selfless service to others is recognized here, and deeply appreciated. It is you who make the world a beautiful place to live in.

With love & light always,

Susie

CONTENTS

ROCK YOUR ROOKIE YEAR IN REAL ESTATE

Foreword

So, you want to be a REALTOR®?   Have your schedule all to yourself, make a lot of money quickly, be your own boss....live the dream? ABSOLUTELY YES! Guess what the truth is?   We all want that, but only a few really get there. This is a roadmap to help you make your real estate dreams a reality. Rock Your Rookie Year in Real Estate reveals successful secrets and pitfalls to avoid that I encountered along my way to starting out with success, combined with top tips and best practices for ramping up your real estate career!

The truth of the matter is being a successful real estate agent takes a lot more than getting your license and signing up with a well-known brokerage. This book is designed to help you think of things and prepare for situations you never imagined you would encounter and need to know. These are situations and practices that are not taught in class and definitely not on the exam. This is real life. I chronicled my entire first year in real estate to bring you first hand experiences of what the learning curve looks like, as well as how to best prepare you for the road ahead!

These are the lessons I have learned from the mistakes I have made. These tips are also the lessons I spent hundreds of thousands of dollars learning in business school and in my master's program – being prepared, being analytical, doing your research and knowing your business (AS WELL AS EVERYONE ELSE's)! Rock Your Rookie Year in Real Estate is designed to prepare you for starting out in real estate...where to focus your time, how to get your first listing and most importantly how to close your first deal.

I am writing this to share with you what I uncovered so that you are prepared and feel confident and successful throughout your rookie year in real estate. Yes, this is a fun, challenging, ever-changing and lucrative business; but you need to have the right knowledge, tools and resources at hand to guide you through it! So here it is!

 Let's get you going!

Here's to your success,

Susie

Introduction

For the past two decades, I have been creating a wonderful life and travelling the world as a professional salesperson. Being successful in sales does not come easily; however, with commitment, determination and some great mentors (including this book), it is absolutely possible. I have attended over 200 sales trainings and have read countless books on the art of selling as well as positive psychology – and believe me, they go hand in hand. While the bulk of my career has been in business to business sales, I write this book to help out everyone who wants to enter their new real estate career with eyes wide open.....and for anyone who wants to wake up their real estate career.

I spent the last year diving into the world of real estate from square one to bring you the best practices and lessons that I have learned in the process of getting myself established as a REALTOR® in my community and getting my real estate business up and running.

This book is designed for you to read either from cover to cover, if you are new to the industry or thinking about becoming a REALTOR®, the pre licensing information may be very helpful to you. If you need some help planning out this career move financially check out my budgeting spreadsheets. Wherever you are, there is a best practice (or several) that you can try out in your own business. I wish you all the best and tremendous success!

A special thank you to all my teachers and co-workers who shared their vast knowledge of this fascinating and lucrative real estate world with me! Your insight, expertise and decades of practice in this field has been fruitful and rewarding; and now others can share in the success that we have experienced!

"Real estate cannot be lost or stolen,

nor can it be carried away.

Purchased with common sense,

paid in full, and managed with reasonable care,

it is about the safest investment in the world".

– Franklin D. Roosevelt
(1882-1945)

Chapter One

Pre-Licensure

PRE-LICENSURE

Define Your Purpose

What is my purpose? And why do I need to have a purpose? My purpose is to become a real estate agent. Isn't that enough? That is certainly true, but your purpose goes beyond that...it is your second and third level questions of "why". Take some time to ask yourself "what are your reasons for wanting to move into real estate"? Why do something different and make a life change? Before you start any new chapter of your life, you need to be clear on why you are making the changes you are making.

Some of the reasons people get into real estate include:

- To provide for your family.
- Because you want to help others.
- Because you love to interact with people.
- To do creative work.
- To work on your own schedule.
- To save for a wedding.
- To leverage your network and social circles.
- To make enough money to purchase your own house.
- To pay for your child's education.
- As a side hustle to your "regular job".
- To build wealth.
- To have uncapped earning potential.

There are hundreds of other reasons why people embark on a career in real estate, so take some time to ask yourself this question. Why do I want to become a real estate agent? Once you have figured out your why, write it down in the space below or someplace where you can easily access it.

My reason to become a real estate agent is:

_____

_____

_____

_____

_____

_____

_____

The reason I am having you do this is because you will be faced with many challenges as you learn this trade. The ups and downs are frequent, so having your purpose close to you will remind you of why you are doing this. Your purpose will help keep you on track and moving towards your goals. And will help keep you focused on what matters most!

Your purpose will change over time, so make it a point to revisit this at least twice a year. As you learn more, your life evolves and you have more experience, your why may change. I recently came across my resume from 2003 - yes 16 years ago - and my purpose and mission are exactly the same today as it was then: "to let the world know that you can make a living doing what you love." I am so honored to be able to help you on your path to real estate success!

Let's Get Licensed!

Select a Pre-Licensure Course

You have decided to give real estate a try and get your real estate license. Now what? Well first of all, you need to enroll in some classroom or online training and prepare for the exam.

Where do I find a class? A quick google search of your area with keywords "real estate" and "pre license course" and the name of your town should bring up a few options. Or if you prefer to see people face to face, consider stopping into a local real estate office and asking them where the classes are offered. I based mine off of the schedule and the cost (they do vary tremendously). For instance, some classes are a weekend class and others are stretched over several months. Some courses are in the morning, others in the evening to accommodate those who have full time day jobs. In my area Jack Conway is a large reputable brokerage, so I decided to enroll in their school. They have several different options for course study and were flexible if I needed to swap out a day class for an evening class and even let me swap out locations. I think very highly of them and would absolutely recommend anyone who has a Jack Conway office near them, to give them a call.

Dearborn Real Estate Prep was the textbook used in my class and I studied it inside and out. You see, I took the class 3 times…. once when I was 18 years old and in college as a favor for a friend in the summertime. I sat through a grueling class that at the time I had little interest in, just a vague curiosity. After graduating and having a few years out in the working world, I again enrolled in the class….at age 26. I had already worked as a Publicist for the Monomoy Music Record Label, a Boutique Manager for a Luxury Women's Clothing Store, St. John and had worked in finance for the Ritz Carlton Hotels of Boston. I was seeing what changes were occurring in the City of Boston and how the façade of the city was transitioning and I wanted in on the action! So, I took the class over a weekend, studied a little….and this time I took the test. I passed the state portion of the exam but not the federal…I was crushed and felt like my only alternative was to become a lawyer. Then I would automatically become a real estate agent.

I hung it up and opted instead for a career in software sales and a Master's in Holistic Leadership…. yet real estate was still calling my name so, at age 38, I resolved to get my license once and for all! I enrolled in a longer class…the first two were all weekend crash courses…now I gave myself a month to absorb all the information and pass the test. I finished classes with Jack Conway and immediately signed up for the test.

Every teacher will tell you to take the exam right away while the information is fresh in your mind! You may feel like you are not ready, but that's mostly the case in life. The riches go to those who show up and face that fear instead of putting things off. I took the test at the first available appointment and this time passed the Federal but not the State. I went home somewhat discouraged but determined! You see, a big part of real estate is passing the test!

Go figure! Better yet go study!

I got in my car and thought…is this worth it? I have failed this test 2 times now, maybe that is a sign. Then I remembered something Headmaster Michael Contompasis from my high school Boston Latin School had once told me:" anyone can master a subject. It is just a matter of time and effort". So, I dialed the exam registration number and signed up immediately for the next test offering. When I got home, I sat down and read the state book cover to cover in one afternoon sitting on the beach. The next day, I went in to retake the state portion of the exam and passed the test! I faced my fears and prevailed! I now have my real estate salesperson license at last…two decades later! Success comes to those who persist.

The reason I shared all of that with you is that it is never too late to try something that interests you or is calling to you. What's that quote *"in the end the only chances we regret are the ones we never took"*?

So why not just give it a try. Real Estate is one of the only flexible careers where you can define how you approach and build out your business...and there are several facets to real estate that you can specialize in like new construction, buyers agents, sellers agents, corporate real estate, condos, real estate finance, photography, staging...the opportunities are endless! Trust your instincts and never give up!

Where is class offered?

To find a class near you, do a google search of "real estate classes" in your area. You should come up with several options. Or begin to notice the real estate offices as you drive around town or in your city. The real estate schools near me are mostly on main roads and post signs or boards announcing when the next classes are being offered.

Give them a call or stop in and speak with them. Get all the details of when the class is being offered, how much it costs, how much work is needed to be done outside of class, etc...and see if you can make it work in your schedule. Sometimes, you just need to sign up and let the rest fall in place. If the rest doesn't fall in place, well that is when you have to take a look at how you are spending your time and start to prioritize. Get some help with the kids, at work, ask for a loan, whatever your current commitments are...and make space for class time. Invest in yourself and your future!

For me teaching style and learning format is crucial. There is nothing worse than being interested in a subject, but not being able to learn it because of a disconnect like language or accents, teaching styles or pace of the class. It is important that I can connect with, understand, and learn from my teacher. If you are like me, it may make sense to sit in on a class or interview some instructors over the phone or in person. If they are not available, google them and read some reviews from their other students.

Ask them tough questions you want answers to. What is your teaching style? Are there online modules? Will I have to be in a classroom for each class? What happens if I miss a class? Can I speak with someone who took your class before? What is your success rate? What percentage of your students pass the exam on the first take? You are paying money for this, so treat it like your job already. I like an animated instructor who weaves in real life examples...but not too many as I don't want to be in class all day long. The test is pretty rigid, so it is also important that the instructor stick with the program.

Select a Class

First, look up your state's requirements. I have provided you with links to each state's real estate board in the section "Real Estate resource links by state" for you to get started. Each state has different exams, requirements, costs and rules for obtaining your license to sell real estate. The National Association of REALTOR®s directories https://www.nar.REALTOR/directories will point you in the right direction. Some states require classroom time prior to taking the exam while others may allow for an online course before you are licenses. Check with your state's real estate board to see what the requirements are.

Figure out how you best learn...morning, nights, or maybe you just need to squeeze in class with the other hundred things on your schedule. Find a class that suits your schedule and learning style. Some people pick up information quickly, so they can take a weekend class and then study on their own. I did that and it didn't work for me. As you know, I passed the state but not the federal exam, and the federal portion is basically what the class focuses on.

There are classes offered once a week over a series of weeks. Taking the class over a series of weeks, I found worked best for my learning style. I was able to focus fully on my class for a few hours once a week and then spend the rest of the week reading through material or practicing some exams – yeah right! I was dreaming of how much money I would make and running numbers on possible commissions. Ready, fire, aim! That is where FOCUS comes in.

There are no commissions without the license and the brokerage, so be sure to show up for class! We will discuss time management further on in the book, but for now, just please be on time to class and ready to learn.

You have a ton of information to master in a very short amount of time; so pay attention, do your homework, take the practice exams, use an app, there are some good ones out there ...like "Upward Mobility" or "Real Estate Exam Prep for Dummies".

How many careers can you think of that you can be licensed and start earning commission for an investment of under $1000 and training in under 2 months? Hardly any! Most professions require years and years of classroom training: Bachelor's Degrees, Master's Degrees or Doctoral degrees in order to even start making money. These professionals are then hundreds of thousands of dollars in student loan debt before they can even apply for a job in their chosen field. In this profession of real estate, you have the chance to get up and running for only a few hundred dollars.

Be aware not to waste your own time and money. You do not need to put yourself in a poor position financially....so please for the couple of weeks or months you are in class, make a commitment to be there, be fully present and ready to learn and absorb as much information as you can. In addition to all this, interact in class. Ask your teacher questions, set up office hours with them for some extra help or guidance, talk to other REALTOR®s, just start to plug into the field. Start thinking and acting like a real estate agent and by ALL means...

Get yourself in the game!

"Preparation for life is so important.

Luck is what happens when preparedness meets opportunity.

Opportunity is all around us.

Are you prepared?"

- Earl Nightingale

Scheduling the Exam (PSI)

Scheduling your exam through PSI (this is for the State of MA) please click on the links below to access your own state's exam link.

Scheduling and Rescheduling: https://candidate.psiexams.com/catalog/fti_agency_license_details.jsp?fromwhere=findtest&testid=4460#

How do I schedule a PSI exam?

For most test programs, PSI provides two easy methods to schedule test appointments:

Online at www.psiexams.com

Phone by calling our Candidate Service Center 1-800-733-9267

What information should I be prepared to provide when I schedule my appointment?

When you schedule your appointment, you should be prepared to provide any of the following information:

The name used to schedule your appointment must exactly match the name shown on your identification. At a minimum, the identification must be a valid, government-issued ID that shows your name in the English alphabet, your signature, your photograph.

Your Social Security, or Licensing Authority/Sponsor issued I.D. Number.

Contact phone numbers - If there is an unexpected event, we will use these numbers to contact you.

Mailing address - Please provide the address to which you would like your score report or other important information mailed.

Exam title. Eligibility information, if required.

E-mail address - Once again for contact purposes, this is often the fastest and most effective means of communication. Many licensing authorities or sponsors require e-mail contact information for registration.

Method of payment.

How can I find out where a test center is located?

www.psiexams.com has a list of testing centers where you may take your exam. Be sure to choose your Licensing Authority/Sponsor name from the drop down menu for an accurate list. Your exam Candidate Information Bulletin will also have a list of locations where your exam is administered.

Can I cancel and/or reschedule my test appointment via the PSI Web site?

Many test appointments can be cancelled and/or rescheduled through the PSI Website. Typically we allow you to schedule 1 day prior if space is available and we require 2 business days to reschedule your exam without penalty. Check your Candidate Information Bulletin for your program's particular rescheduling rules.

How long will it take for my eligibility or authorization to test to be downloaded into the system so that I can schedule an appointment to test?

Please note that not all Licensing Authorities/Sponsors require eligibility to take their exam, therefore, you may be able to test immediately. For those programs requiring eligibility, the files are downloaded and test appointment scheduling is available within 24-48 hours of receiving authorization from the licensing authority.

Why would my local test center tell me that they don't schedule appointments?

The testing centers' primary purpose is to administer exams. Candidates should visit our website or contact our Candidate Service Center to schedule an exam appointment. Test center staff are not able to schedule appointments for their test center under any circumstances.

How do I obtain the appointment date and time I want to take my exam?

When you go to our website or speak to a representative from our Candidate Service Center you will be asked to provide your preferred test date. The first available time slot on that date will be offered to you. If your preferred appointment date is not available, a Candidate Service Center representative will work with you to identify a convenient appointment date.

My appointment is scheduled for today, however the testing center is closed. What should I do?

In rare cases weather or an emergency forces a test center closure. If this happens you will be contacted by the PSI rescheduling department within 24-48 hours to reschedule your appointment. We apologize for any inconvenience. You may also call 800-733-9267 for information. Real time site information is posted at psiexams.com

How far in advance must you schedule an exam?

Exam sessions are available at least 6 weeks in advance. You will have the best opportunity to schedule your preferred date if you contact us 4-6 weeks prior to your preferred date.

Is licensure the same for every state?

No! These rules will vary by state that you live in or that you choose to sell real estate in. Please refer to the list below of all 50 states in the United States with the links out ot their Real Estate Boards or Licensing Board. Click on these links to learn more about what the requirements are for your particular state. Each licensing board should have a phone number for you to call and ask questions to. If not, send me a message through www.SusieGillis.com indicating what state you live in and what state you will be selling in and I will direct you to where you need to go

Real Estate Resource Links by State:

Alabama	https://arec.alabama.gov/arec/
Alaska	https://www.commerce.alaska.gov/web/cbpl/Profession alLicensing/RealEstateCommission.aspx
Arkansas	https://arec.arkansas.gov/
Arizona	http://re.state.az.us/Lic/QualifyObtainLicFaqs.aspx
California	http://dre.ca.gov/
Colorado	https://colorado.gov/pacific/dora/division-real-estate
Connectic ut	https://www.licensetutor.com/real-estate-license-requirements/connecticut/
Delaware	https://dpr.delaware.gov/boards/realestate/ressalesper son/
Florida	https://www.stateofflorida.com/real-estate-licensing.aspx
Georgia	https://www.grec.state.ga.us/
Hawaii	http://cca.hawaii.gov/reb/
Idaho	https://irec.idaho.gov/

Illinois	https://www.idfpr.com/DRE.asp
Indiana	https://www.in.gov/pla/real.htm
Iowa	https://plb.iowa.gov/
Kansas	http://www.krec.ks.gov/licensing
Kentucky	https://krec.ky.gov/Pages/default.aspx
Louisiana	http://www.lrec.state.la.us/home/
Maryland	http://www.dllr.state.md.us/license/mrec/
Maine	https://www.maine.gov/pfr/professionallicensing/professions/real_estate/
Massachusetts	https://www.mass.gov/orgs/board-of-registration-of-real-estate-brokers-and-salespersons
Michigan	https://www.michigan.gov/snyder/0,4668,7-277-57738_57679_57726-250090--,00.html
Minnesota	https://mn.gov/commerce/licensees/real-estate/
Mississippi	http://www.mrec.state.ms.us/
Missouri	https://pr.mo.gov/realestate.asp

Montana	http://boards.bsd.dli.mt.gov/rre
Nebraska	http://www.nrec.ne.gov/
Nevada	http://red.nv.gov/
New Hampshire	https://www.oplc.nh.gov/real-estate-commission/index.htm
New Jersey	https://www.state.nj.us/dobi/division_rec/licensing/online_Instructions/licSearch.html
New Mexico	http://www.rld.state.nm.us/boards/Real_Estate_Commission.aspx
New York	https://www.dos.ny.gov/licensing/fees_terms.html
North Carolina	https://www.ncrec.gov/Licensing/Licensees
North Dakota	https://www.realestatend.org/
Ohio	https://com.ohio.gov/REAL/
Oklahoma	https://www.ok.gov/OREC/
Oregon	https://www.oregon.gov/REA/pages/index.aspx

Pennsylvania	https://www.pals.pa.gov/#/page/default
Rhode Island	http://www.dbr.state.ri.us/divisions/commlicensing/real estate.php
South Carolina	http://www.llr.state.sc.us/pol/rec/
South Dakota	http://dlr.sd.gov/realestate/default.aspx
Tennessee	https://www.tn.gov/commerce/regboards/trec.html
Texas	https://www.trec.texas.gov/
Utah	https://realestate.utah.gov/realestate/index.html
Vermont	https://www.sec.state.vt.us/professional-regulation/list-of-professions/real-estate-commission.aspx
Virginia	http://www.dpor.virginia.gov/Boards/Real-Estate/
Washington	https://www.dol.wa.gov/business/realestate/realestate commission.html
West Virginia	https://rec.wv.gov/Pages/default.aspx
Wisconsin	https://dsps.wi.gov/pages/RulesStatutes/RealEstate.asp

	X
Wyoming	http://realestate.wyo.gov/

Taking the Exam

The real estate licensure exam is tricky, and it should be! People will be trusting you with the most expensive investment of their lives, so you want to train yourself to become familiar with errors and opportunities. Just like you will encounter in the field, you need to be sharp and looking out for errors that may appear on the exam. Several answers appear to be the correct one, so be sure to read the questions carefully, so study up!

Make flash cards. Take a stack of index cards and write out a question on one side and the answer on the other side. Make it fun and pair up with a friend in class to keep each other honest...or just go through all these questions one by one until you know them all by heart. The practice will help you get in exam taking mode, plus you have the benefit of both reading and writing the questions and answers so that they sink into your memory.

Use the app - Co-Co E Learning has a Real Estate Exam Prep 2019 app available for your smartphone or ipads. Install the app and drill yourself on the questions whenever you have a free moment. Instead of scrolling mindlessly through facebook and Instagram, open up your real estate test taking app and review some questions. Waiting in line at the grocery store or dentist's office, go through a few questions so that the information is committed to memory.

Take the practice exams...whatever it takes! You want to STUDY until you know the material like a champ. Learn it so that you know it so well it is insulting taking the exam. Confidence is a huge piece of testing taking, however when you compare preparedness with confidence you are unstoppable.

Class is almost over and I have been keeping up with the practice tests and doing all the review questions. Am I ready to take the test? Experts say it is best to take the exam within the first week or two after your classes are complete. I know you may want to set aside a month or two to study even more, but your best bet is to jump right in. It never really felt like the right time for me, but I learned to quiet those voices of doubt in my head and be brave.

Schedule your exam time and take the test shortly after you finish class.... the info is fresher in your mind at that time.

Or your other options are:

1) Keep paying to retake the exam = your time and money wasted.

2) Become an attorney = Yes this actually crossed my mind... and by being an attorney you automatically get your real estate license.

3) Find another profession.

Take this Quizlet to work on some of your real estate math formulas: https://quizlet.com/29471348/real-estate-math-formulas-helper-flash-cards/

The exam is in a format that is a multiple-choice format, however the way the questions are written is tricky and the answer options often times appear like there can be more than one correct answer. That being said, it is imperative you read and re-read the question in order to be sure you clearly understand the questions properly before jumping ahead with an answer.

When test taking, especially timed tests; I have learned it is best to read through the exam at a good pace and answer the questions you absolutely know the answer to and mark the ones you are not so sure of or that need more time to complete. This way you at least have all the ones you know answered – the point is not to get a perfect score, rather to pass the exam. If you get a perfect score, that's great but not the main goal here.

It is also important to take timed practice exams. Timed tests can be mentally rigorous, so just as an athlete would train for a competition or game, you need to train your brain to endure this exam. Build up your attention, stamina and focus gradually; until you are comfortable going through the whole exam at one sitting. I know when taking the test, I was drained after completing the national portion of the exam and didn't have enough stamina to focus on the state portion of the exam or the brain power I needed to pass it. So be aware of that factor, it can save you time and money in the long run from having to retake the exam.

Some test taking tips include:

√ Get a good night's sleep the night before.

√ Have a good meal, but don't overeat.

√ Give yourself time to get to the exam, find and pay for parking, and find the office where the test is being administered.

√ Read through the questions carefully. Be sure you are clear on what is being asked.

√ Answer the questions you absolutely know first and mark the ones you are unsure of.

√ Skip questions you are not positive about.

√ Memorize formulas like 1 acre = 43,560 sf

√ Be mindful of your time. If you are nearing the end of your allotted time, speed it up a bit. It's better to attempt an answer than to keep it blank.

√ If you don't know a math answer, plug in all the answers to see which one fits the question.

√ Stay focused on your own progress. You are in a room with several other test takers of all sorts. They may have a totally different exam than you are working on, so stay focused on you and your progress.

Your goal is to feel ready and refreshed prior to going in to sit for the exam. Make sure you read the exam booklet so you know all the rules and requirements of what you can and cannot bring into the exam. Map out your route and be sure you leave yourself enough time for traffic and parking. Give yourself ample time to find parking and battle some morning traffic.

I took my exam in the city of Boston and I could not find parking at all. The lot was full and there were no meters available on the street. It was just as stressful getting myself to the exam as it was taking the exam!

The point is you do not want to be flustered and late for the exam....you want to be in a great mind frame; relaxed and confident!

Practice Tests

To assure you pass the exam on the first try (which isn't necessary but would be amazing!), get into test taking mode as early as possible.

See what my friends at www.test.com have to say AND be sure to click their link to sign up for some FREE practice exams online: https://www.tests.com/practice/Real-Estate-Agent-License-Practice-Test

"Generally, you can expect that your state real estate agent license exam will consist of 80-100 multiple-choice questions about general real estate concepts and 60-80 questions specific to state licensing laws. Most states administer the tests in two parts, and require that the candidate pass both. The general part of the exam is broken into several categories, similar to the categories you will see in the samples".

If you want to take your test prep further, for under $30 they offer access to the full 300 question practice exam.

Resources like this a GOLD! They are written by real estate professionals who teach the pre licensure course and are designed to be a close resemblance of the actual test. By logging in at least twice a day for the 2 weeks leading up to your exam date, you will literally train yourself to be solidly prepared to ace the exam. And there is no cost to you! How amazing is that? Anyone who shares information like this to help others is an angel in my eyes. Selfless service makes the world go around!

One trick I use is to mark the questions I do not know. Then I go back and leave them marked when I take the exam again. I redo the entire exam if I did not get a 100%. The ones I know, great I know them, but if I am remotely unsure about a question, I will mark it so that I can find out the exact answer and be crystal clear about what the right answer is.

Chapter Two

Broker Up!

BROKER UP!

Selecting a brokerage office to work with

Now that you are a real estate salesperson, you need a place to park your license!

Maybe you already have a real estate brokerage in mind, however, now that you have your license, it is time to decide who you want to align yourself with.   (Some of the more ambitious folks may have already started this process while obtaining your license, or maybe you have a friend you want to work with and will go to that office). At any rate, it is time to select a real estate brokerage to partner up with. Sorry to say, just because you have your license does not mean you can go out and sell houses all on your own. Transactions occur from broker to broker, and at this point, you are not a broker.

So, pick a great one! Select one that makes you feel your best! That has great energy, fun events, great people and technology! Look at how successful Mauricio Umansky has been with his AGENCY! In a few short years, his passion, eye for design and work ethic has built his company to 25 locations! Think about it, your brokerage is how you will get paid... and how you will set the foundation for your real estate career and your professional brand ...and as you know all the money flows through the brokerage.

"It takes 20 years to build a reputation

and five minutes to ruin it.

If you think about that,

you'll do things differently."

-   Warren Buffett

Choosing the brokerage office to partner with is a critical piece in establishing yourself as a real estate agent. This will be your home base, your peers and people who will support you, so choose wisely. If you select an office and do not feel like they are a good fit, I would say give it a couple of months. New things always feel uncomfortable so give it some time - often difficult and uncomfortable people & situations tend to teach us the best lessons in life! If after a few months, it still isn't right, look for another brokerage or office to team up with. Start interviewing new ones and look for a place you feel is a better fit for your needs.

Often times agents will change brokerages within their first 6 months. Or perhaps you have been with your broker for years and they are no longer offering you what another brokerage can — maybe there is a better split of the commission, or better marketing resources, keep your eyes and ears open because nothing is forever.

Some of the things you want to look for in an office and some questions you will want to have answered:

☐ How long have they been in business?

☐ What is their reputation in the local market?

☐ Are they a well-known brand?

☐ Are they a national brand that pays for prime advertising?

☐ Do I see their ads during important sports events, or awards ceremonies?

☐ Are they a household name?

☐ What is the commission percentage they will pay you?

    ✓ Is it a sliding percentage scale...the more volume the higher the commission % ?

    ✓ Is it a flat percentage rate?

☐ What sort of training or classes do they offer?

    ✓ Is there ongoing training?

    ✓ Is there virtual and classroom training?

☐ What resources do they have for you?

    ✓ computers

    ✓ printers

    ✓ phone lines, internet, email & fax

    ✓ personalized riders

    ✓ business cards

    ✓ paid direct mailing and postage expenses

    ✓ promotional materials to hand out

☐ Do they have virtual office?

    ✓ all your forms and tools online for you to access anywhere?

☐ How successful are their agents?

    ✓ Are they making enough to pay their bills?

    ✓ How many agents earning over $250k?

    ✓ Are the agents working more than 60-80 hours per week?

    ✓Are the agents living an affluent lifestyle?

✓ Do they give back to their communities?

☐ Are there any fees for joining the brokerage agency?

☐ Is there an office fee?

☐ Do you have to rent space?

All of this needs to be accounted for. Some brokerage firms take a percentage off the top of each deal to pay for office expenses, advertising, supplies, etc. What works best for you? Go around to several different brokerages and learn as much as you can from them. Maybe you attend one of their meetings to see how management operates and trains their agents. Find out as much as you can because you are laying the foundation of your real estate career on this brokerage. This is your cornerstone.

☐ How many agents do they have?

☐ What are their agents like?

   ✓ Are they nice people?

   ✓ Are they willing to answer a question for you or help?

   ✓ Would one be willing to mentor you?

   ✓ Ask if you could ride around and shadow an agent for a day or two.

☐ Are their agents ethical?

☐ Are their agents tenured?

Tenured means have they been around for a while or do they turn over quickly and leave...and if they do, why is this happening?

Interview some of the agents and see why they chose that particular brokerage and be sure to interview your manager. This person will be your lifeline to your success starting out, so be sure that your manager is someone who you want to work with and learn from.

Observe their management style and see if it is in alignment with yours. Do they call when they say they will? Are they accountable for their actions and what they promise you? Are they good people and do you like them? You will be spending quite a bit of time with your manager so make sure you like them and can have fun with them!

You also want to research and get comfortable with the style business the brokerage is. Perhaps it is a mom and pop small business where you have a lot of contact and interaction with other agents which may be a good thing; or you may want a brokerage that is part of a national or international brand that has the corporate backbone to support you in your learning and set up of your business.

There are even virtual offices now that offer very high commission splits but zero office resources. All of them are great and agents have success in each of those formats. You need to realize what feels right for you!

Being a real estate agent or a REALTOR® is being in business for yourself. That being said, selecting the right office can make it a whole lot easier for you starting out by having the right people, systems, and tools at your fingertips.

Do I need to become a REALTOR®?

Not all real estate agents are REALTORS®. That is right! Often times people will mix up these terms and use them incorrectly. Just because you have your real estate salesperson license does not mean that you are a REALTOR®.

REALTOR® or real estate salesperson that is the question?

Deciding to become a REALTOR® may be a personal decision, or it may be a requirement of the brokerage you choose to partner with. The National Association of REALTOR®s is a member-based organization that abides by high ethical standards and a commitment to continuous education. These are the people who march on Capitol Hill to lobby and protects the rights of all people in the real estate industry. They create positive impacts in their communities and throughout this country.

Per the www.NAR.REALTOR® website, "The National Association of REALTORS® is America's largest trade association, representing 1.3 million members, including NAR's institutes, societies, and councils, involved in all aspects of the residential and commercial real estate industries.

Our membership is composed of residential and commercial brokers, salespeople, property managers, appraisers, counselors, and others engaged in the real estate industry. Members belong to one or more of approximately 1,200 local associations/boards and 54 state and territory associations of REALTORS®."

There is a fee associated with membership and there are many benefits to becoming a member such as continuous education classes, master mind classes, leadership training and giving back to the communities around you. Additionally, there are several other member benefits such as leadership opportunities, or direct volunteer opportunities within the community. Several brokerages require that their agents belong to NAR and become a REALTOR®. So, check with your office to see what they require.

Costs to build your real estate business

Save up because 99% of brokerages operate on a commission only pay structure. Unless you work for Red Fin or have some other arrangement, most brokerages pay you only when you close a deal ...and it can take upwards of a month after the deal closes to see your portion of the commission.

Getting a deal takes time and money so I will repeat = save up folks! It can take up to year to get your first deal signed and your commission paid so save up at LEAST a year's living expenses plus the costs I will outline for getting your business launched. It is always good to have a little more tucked away because you may see that rainy day. If you need to move home or get a roommate...do it! Money can be tight, so it is better to be prepared. You may decide to teach, take a part time job waitressing or tending bar to keep the money flowing and keep your name out there in public. Do it!

Budgeting your first year in real estate

If you have read this far in the book, it tells me that you are serious about real estate as your career and want to do everything possible to make your start a very successful one. As with all startup businesses - and yes, you are on your way to running your very own start up business in real estate - you need to budget and project out what your costs will be. If you are independently wealthy and do not have to think about budgets, consider giving back and creating a scholarship at your local brokerage, high school or college for someone who wants to pursue real estate as a career but does not have the means.

Whatever the case may be, below is what most agents spend money on starting off in real estate and in years to come. Yes, there are several costs to become an agent and build your real estate business, so listen up!

Class fees: this is your tuition for classroom training to prepare you to take your real estate exam. This fee includes the instructor's fees and your required textbooks. Pre-licensure class costs about $200-400 depending on your location*.

*Check Groupon to see if there are discounted classes offered if money is really tight for you.

License fees: this is the cost for your real estate salesperson license. This cost varies by state and can be found online on your state's website. In my state of Massachusetts, it is no more than $150. The license is prorated based upon your date of birth (which is when the license renews) and the date you passed the exam. So if you passed the exam on your birthday, it would be the full $150; versus if you took the exam 6 months after your birthday.

Books: pre license textbooks are often included in the cost of your classroom training. However, if purchased separately, they can run about $150.

Exam: (test) fees vary by state. They are $54 (as of this writing in the state of Massachusetts: https://candidate.psiexams.com/catalog/fti_agency_license_details.jsp? fromwhere=findtest&testid=4460). Reference PSI registration details in the back of this book.

Exam retake fees: These fees vary by state as well. They are $54 (each time in the state of MA; this cost differs state to state) please refer to the links in the back of this book to your state real estate boards for exact figures.

REALTOR® fees (yes this makes you an ethical agent and a member of the National Association of REALTORS®). By becoming involved with the local and national resource, you will receive access to great training resources. This is especially helpful if the brokerage you partner with does not have much to offer from training, you can rely on your REALTOR® regional office for training. It is a wonderful way to network and meet other agents. They are the ones with whom you will be working with so consider getting on board. This can run upwards of $600 per year for local, state and national REALTOR® dues.

MLS Fees: This is where you will find your business and do the majority of your research. The MLS is an online service that you pay for quarterly. I pay $87 per quarter to gain access to MLS (multiple listing service) and to add listings to the MLS (Multiple Listing Service).

Office fees: Some brokerage offices include their fee in the commission breakout. Check with your manager to see what office expenses will be. Some brokers take a percentage of your commission off the top from a sale to cover their office and marketing expenses. You may also want to set up a home office – so a printer, laptop, paper, etc. This can run about $2500 on the low end (but is also a tax write off for those who itemize their deductions...talk to your accountant about the benefits). If you have a home office, you may be able to deduct your home office costs on your taxes. Be sure to check with your tax accountant for details.

Transportation expenses: This is the cost for gas to get you to and from all of your showings and client meetings. Do you own a car? Use Uber? Driving can be expensive, especially if you are paying for parking in a city or gas to travel many miles out in the countryside. Be sure to keep good records of miles driven and cost for gas each trip. That way when you go to do your taxes, you can write your car usage, repairs and gas used for real estate off as a business expense. Consider using software like Quickbooks Intuit to track your expenses.

Taxes & insurances: As a real estate agent you are an "independent contractor" to the brokerage you partner with. So unlike being an employee where you are paid a salary, receive health insurance and other employee benefits, 401k, and taxes withheld for state and federal tax filings - as an independent contractor you just receive a check for the commission you earned for your real estate sales transactions. A lump sum. That is it. It is totally up to you to source your own health & wellness insurance, pay your taxes to the state, local and federal governments and put money aside for your retirement.

More tools to invest in for your real estate career:

Smart Phone: Smartphone preferably and remember to ALWAYS ANSWER YOUR PHONE! This is your lifeline to success, so make sure your phone works and you have great network coverage. I am on the phone all the time. For me, texting is my #1 mode of communication, then email and the phone are tied for #2.

Your smartphone should also have a great camera….

And use it! Take a photo of the exterior of homes you are looking at with buyers. You will be looking at hundreds of houses and they will start to get confusing. Snap a quick photo to help place it in your mind. Additionally, if you need to clarify a property for a client; you can send them a quick photo of the home in question to jog their memory.

To save money, I will use my phone to take great photos for my listings. Photography is something I excel at, so it is easy for me to find the right angles and show the best of the home. I went with the Samsung Galaxy Note 8 in order to have THE BEST pictures and it works great! I take great pictures that accurately depict the properties I am representing.

If you are not into photography, hire a professional. Trust me, people buy from pictures, so make sure they are beautiful depictions of the homes you are representing! It is well worth it paying $100-$1,000 for a real estate photographer. It does eat up your profits (or comes out of pocket if you don't sell it), but it is a necessity in real estate. Some brokerages will cover your professional photography fees so be sure to ask up front what expenses the brokerage covers!

GPS: Your navigation system is key! You absolutely need to know where you are going. And you need to know how long it will take to get there - in traffic and otherwise. Waze works awesome in my area and helps me avoid traffic, roadwork, slowdowns, accidents, etc. In cases where it is a very important meeting I will often times do a dry run the day or two before just to get more familiar with the roadways and the neighborhoods of the property I am listing. Waze works best for me now, as it takes into account traffic, etc. I use google maps as my backup.

Transportation: Your mode of instant transportation will vary depending on your geographic location. Some real estate agents will use Uber or public transportation; others will walk, take a boat or a helicopter to get to where they need to be. But for the majority, I can assume you will be using a car. That being the case, make sure the car has gas in the tank and it is clean and neat should you be driving your client around. If Uber is your mode of transportation, be sure they are reliable and build in traffic time. When a client or potential client calls, you have to be ready to go...right away! If you need to hop on a bicycle, do it! Ask for a ride if necessary...whatever it is, just be there on or before time!

Laptop computer: you will need access to a computer or if you plan on being in the office just use one there. See the list above. There are so many options out now from chromebooks to more powerful gaming computers, buy the one that will allow you access to your files and that load up quickly. Laptops range from $250 - $3000+. I would get something with at least 8 GB or 12GB RAM and good graphic display.

Printer: most of the documents you use are available digitally, however not all of your clients will be computer savvy so you need to be able to print out documents for them when needed. Your office may have a printer, or you can always use a Staples or office supply store or even your local library for your printing needs. But, if you do buy a home printer, be sure the printer has a scanner function. I love my Pixma! Average is $300.

Headshot: This is the cost to have your professional headshots (photographs) taken. If you are starting off on a budget, have a friend or someone you trust take your photo for you. Be sure your photo is clear, focuses on you and truly represents you! Ideally there will be a solid background so that the image focuses on you and nothing else. Dress professionally and if needed have someone style you hair and makeup (or just do it yourself). This photo will go out on listings, your business cards, etc so be sure you like this photo!   Professional photographers can run $200-$500+ per sitting.

Business cards: This is one of your top tools of the trade. This card will have your photo, your brokerage address, your agent license #, phone number, fax number, email and website. You want people to be able to get in touch with you any way possible. Check to see if you brokerage will pay for your first set of business cards. If not, I have used zazzle.com and uprinting.com to have business cards made for under $40. Check around to see who has the best quality and can deliver them quickly.

Website: So many transactions are happening online these days. You need to have a strong web presence. A great website is mandatory. Most brokerages will set you up with one, but you will want to personalize it to make it stand out from the rest. If you are web savvy, go to godaddy.com and buy your domain. I would suggest you buy your name if you can. Some sites I have used to build websites pretty easily are wix.com and weebly.com. I bought my name domain and pointed it to my brokerage site: check out my website at www.SusieGillis.com

Flashlight: Why do I need a flashlight? Some of the houses will have the electricity turned off. Or you may have to show a house after dark. Having a flashlight there to help out with lockbox is key. However, layer in a cold or rainy winters night, plus the darkness, plus the flashlight, plus talking to your client and keeping cool; well that will take practice. You may also need to look into attics and basements, so it is always great to keep a flashlight on hand. Some agents carry a large metal flashlight.

Electronic measurer: This will help you determine the square footage of a home in a snap! I bought a Bosch laser distance measurer from Home Depot for up to 120 feet. The thing is awesome! You literally hold it against a wall press a button and the laser points to the opposite wall reading the distance. It can even store measurements to make it even easier to use. This is a life saver is you have a listing and need to measure out the rooms and square footage of a home. Trust me, this is worth EVERY PENNY. About $115 (sometimes you can get them on sale).

Chapter Three

Leverage A Mentor

LEVERAGE A MENTOR

"If you cannot see where you are going,

ask someone who has been there before"

- J Loren Norris

Photo by rawpixel.com from Pexels

Work with a Mentor

Mentors are agents or brokers who have been in the business for a while. They have a firm grasp on their profession, are successful and are willing to cut you in and share their knowledge of how they run their business and became successful. They will show you the ropes. You need to start somewhere, and instead of trying to figure everything out on your own, why not learn from the best? By shadowing seasoned and successful agents, it will save you thousands of dollars and hours and cut your learning curve down significantly.

These people have their real estate businesses up and running and instead of sitting back trying to figure everything out on your own, have a mentor to help get you going! Observe how they operate, maybe ask for a day a week or a couple hours a day to ride along and see how they operate. See how they interact with their clients, how they get deals done. Observe and copy their strategies in order to break the ice in this competitive business. Ask them for help and guidance and in return help them with their open houses, or other marketing help they may need. Who do they go to for help? Who is in their network? Where do their listings come from? Take it all in and start experimenting with the skills picked up from observing and working with your mentor.

Trust me. What you learn and study for the test has very little to do with being an agent. But it is required and the only way you can get in the REALTOR® game.

What can a mentor do for me?

They can fast track you!

Make your life a whole lot easier (or harder during the learning curve)!

Mentors can you the true ins and outs of agent life. Beyond all the information you learned from the test, the real stuff that get you listings and closed deals. The role of every successful agent is to close deals. That is it. A real estate agents' job is solely to bring buyers and sellers together in order to transact the business of real estate exchange from seller to buyer.

However, there are hundreds of things agents do behind the scenes like back office processes. How do I read my contracts? What needs to be signed? Who signs the P&S? What do the attorney's need to review? Or what about how do I change the ink on the printer? Or where are the envelopes to mail a contract? How do I measure out a property? What are the zoning laws? Can this parcel be built on? IS there asbestos in the house? Who can remove this junk car from the yard?

A mentor can show you how to best market yourself. What works in your region? Do you need to invest in a billboard? Should you buy mugs for the local pub with your business card on them? Or maybe join the local NAR chapter to stay plugged in.

A mentor can show you who the key players are in the office. Who is an expert at what part of the business and how they can help (or if they will even help…)? They will show you who you need to partner with outside of the office…attorneys, stagers, photographers, landscapers, movers…the whole shebang! Check out my tribe list for more referral channels.

You are aligning yourself with success and oftentimes your mentor will cut you in on the deals in exchange for your help with open houses, making calls, marketing the property etc…. Think of it as a win- win. You are helping them and they are definitely helping you. In some cases, you may have skills that they do not….like with using apps, building websites, using software, social media, etc , so they can show you what they are experts in and you can help your mentors out in the areas you are an expert.

Combine forces and grow your business!

How do I select a mentor?

You may want to ask your office manager who has mentored new agents before or if they can recommend someone who may be open to mentoring you. In this case, the manager can take the lead and make the introduction for you.

Sometimes a mentor can be the person who brought you on board to the brokerage of your choice. In this case, that person is compensated (often times) on your success. The brokerage will kick them a percentage of your closed sales for them recruiting you! Nothing comes out of your pocket, but the referral agent / mentor gets a bonus for bringing you on board!

Think of someone who has a lot of listings or someone who has been in the business for a long time. Who is that name in the community you want to sell in that everyone thinks of when they think of real estate? THAT is the person who you want to learn from and become.

If your manager is not able to identify a mentor for you, you may want to identify someone who is leading the field, or whose style you would like to emulate and approach them yourself. Give them a call or send them an email asking if they are free for coffee this week or next at 10am. (Always give a time and place when you send out an invitation. It makes it easier for the invitee to say yes!) Let them know that you want to learn from the best and in your opinion, they are the best person to learn from!

Flattery will get you places, trust me...plus you are being truthful! You clearly admire this person, or you wouldn't have chosen them. So be vocal about who you select and why it would mean the world if you could learn from them.

What if I cannot find a Mentor?

Relax, it will all work out! A mentor isn't always someone who is there to meet with you regularly and hold your hand as you cross the street. I found some of my greatest mentors in books, sales trainings, website and by committing to personal growth early on. You can start at any point; and make a promise to yourself that you can and will be successful as a real estate agent and you will find the tools to get yourself there!

Remember in the beginning of the book I wrote about myself and why I wrote this book and what qualifies me for writing this ...it is sales trainings! All those years I didn't have just one mentor, I had hundreds of mentors. I devoured books, attended any and all trainings available to me, did audio courses from Earl Nightingale, Tony Robbins, any and all self-help guru out there. I listened to their tapes (yes Tony Robbins was available on cassette take back in the day), watched their youtube videos, attended their seminars and trainings, and read their books (books are still free at your local library). I studied their techniques and applied them to my philosophies and practices in every sales role I have embarked on - and succeeded in! Low on cash, go to the library and borrow a course, any course and commit yourself to lifelong personal development & learning.

Starting out in your new office

"It's better to hang out with people better than you.

Pick out associates whose behavior is better than yours and you'll drift in that direction."

-Warren Buffett

Photo by Ylanite Koppens from Pexels

Congratulations! You have selected the brokerage you want to work with and signed your life away – your old life that is! Now it is time to move into your new office and embark on your profitable career and get focused on building your successful real estate career.

The new kid.

Yup, that it you! Most likely the seasoned agents have seen tens of ambitious and eager agents come and go through their office like a revolving door. So, you need to stand out in the crowd and make yourself known!

Sometimes it is difficult to make your mark, so one thing that worked really well for me was a letter (or email) of intent. This was a brief letter I sent out to everyone in the office introducing myself. It included who I am, my education, where I came from and it also outlined my goals for myself. What I wanted to achieve and what I expected of myself. This shows you are committed to this career and it also fills in the gaps so people are not talking behind your back or wondering what you are up to or all about. It is spelled out plain and simple. This is your personal manifesto!

Give it a try and begin to carve out your place in the office.

Dear Office,

I am thrilled to be part of this team! A little bit about me, I am Susie Gillis and I am local to this town. I am passionate about helping others and feel called to be in real estate to help people find the home of their dreams and make one of the biggest investments of their lives! From what I have seen we have an incredible roster of agents here and I am eager to learn from all of you! If you need any help please let me know. I am excellent at social media and ready to get started! Here's to our success!

Susie

What is out there?

Get to know your market and the inventory inside and out. The MLS is a good starting point for this. Check it at least once a day EVERY day. But I would suggest checking it out every morning to see the new listings and evening to see what has closed or sold at the very minimum. It is available on your smartphone, so you can access it from wherever you have service. Drive around different neighborhoods, typically when one sign goes up ...others will as well right in the same area. This is especially true when a house sells for a great price, the neighbors all want in on those profits so are eager to sell their homes too!

Office listings, what properties are being represented by the agents and brokers in your office? Are they offering a preview of the property so you can get in and see it before the rest of the agents out there? Check to see if your office has an office listing sheet and be sure to tour all of those properties and speak with the listing agents to learn all that you can about them.

Drive around and look! See what is coming soon, notice who is doing work on their house. Get to know the different communities you will be selling in. Go to the town meetings and start to listen, observe and learn all about what is going on in the towns.

Hi I'm Susie, who are you?

Seems pretty simple, but how many people actually do this? Introduce yourself! Don't wait for someone else to ask, go and say hi! It is so important to get to know all the people in your office. They are the ones you will be learning from and relying on so make sure you go into the office for an hour so each day so that people are seeing you and getting to know you! It is amazing what you will learn just from being within earshot of anyone in the midst of a real estate transaction.

And if you are shy...wear your name badge out and about! People will strike up a conversation with you while getting coffee, etc when they see you are a real estate agent. Everybody has bought, sold or wants to buy or sell their home ...so you always have something in common.

Lunch & learn...I'm in!

ATTEND EVERY OFFICE EVENT THAT YOU CAN. As a new agent, you need to soak up as much information as possible as quickly as possible. What better way of doing this than by surrounding yourself with the professionals in your office! Show them that you are part of the team and you are here to learn! Get to know everyone in your office and let them get to know you. This builds rapport, trust and teamwork. Plus it can be really fun! Maybe even volunteer to plan the next event!

Friends / Family / People in the office – this is where my initial business comes from. Family parties, let everyone know you are in real estate and would LOVE to do business with them. On the ballfield, at the gymnastics meet or on the golf course, waiting in line for coffee or getting take out ...wherever you find yourself, let your friends, acquaintances, new people you meet all know you are a REALTOR® and would love to do business with them. If anyone in their network needs help with real estate, it would be your pleasure to help them. Make sure you give them your card ...and a couple extras!

Tour the properties so you know them well!

Talk with your real estate peers! I see you have a new listing, congrats! Just wondering if you have any appointments scheduled that I can piggyback on one of those to see the listing? That way I can see what is on the market and help you out if you need me to.

Walking into a real estate career of any other career, you have to ramp up as quickly as possible. We live in a highly ultra-competitive workforce, and someone is always on the prowl to capture your client or that listing. Knowing what is out there and available, will help you tremendously when you are standing in the grocery line and someone out of the blue recognizes you as a REATLOR® and asks you about the house up on Elm Street. You definitely want to be able to converse with them professionally and knowledgeably about the property. So, keep your eyes open, and start to build your library of homes.

Attend the Broker Open Houses

These open houses are usually just for real estate agents and brokers. On occasion the listing agent will invite the public to make the most of their time and the market conditions. This is most often done when a house is new to the market or just before it goes to the public for viewing. Brokers are exclusively invited to tour the property before the general public. It is a great way to get to know what's out there, what is available and excellent way to network with other real estate agents and brokers! The goal is to get the house shown and talked about. Any buyers you have that would fit this property, let them know about it! Hopefully, you can get the house sold prior to the open house. As a bonus, often times there is food served or beverages, so come ready to network, learn and enjoy a bite to eat!

Participate in the caravans

These are the weekly tours your office puts together to showcase the homes represented by the agents in your particular office. This is a weekly event with one to as many new houses are listed by the office. This is your chance to see the properties with your peers before the public views it! Like a sneak preview or VIP party!

Make note of the differences between the homes, the prices they are being offered for and any special amenities the houses have. For example: Almost all had garages, or a basement and the one that didn't have a huge brand-new family room addition.

"If only you could sense how important you are

to the lives of those you meet;

how important you can be to people you may never even dream of.

There is something of yourself that you leave

at every meeting with another person."

– Fred Rogers

Interact with people as much as possible

You are a unique and special gift to humankind. Yes, you are! And you have chosen a very special profession. It is an honor to be able to help others fulfill their dreams of homeownership, so treat each person with your complete presence, focus and well intentions.

I have a friend who is so skilled at being present, she listens to each and every word I say and remembers every conversation we have. She is so tapped in and tuned into you, that everything else fades. When I am with her, I feel like I am the only person in the whole world! It is truly a gift and the type of person I aspire to be!

While I am not sure if this is possible all the time, as we only have so much time in the day, it may be something you want to practice with your clients. Especially on first meetings and when you are learning about them and what their real estate needs are. Focus completely in on them. Pay no attention to other distractions, like what you want to say or what information you had planned to give to them. Put all that aside and just tune in 100 percent to your client and listen to them. Place your absolute full attention on them. Give it a try!

Interact with people as much as possible, what does this mean, don't I already do this? Yes, you do, but not as effectively as you could be. You may know hundreds of people and have thousands of followers on social media, but when asked about real estate are you the first name that comes out of their mouth? You need to become TOP OF MIND for all your contacts. By that I mean, friends, family, people in your gym, yoga classes, your mailman, people at the gas station. Get the word out in a professional manner so that next time someone asks them about real estate, your name is the only one they can think of.

There are few feelings worse them learning that your best friend just bought a house from a random real estate agent. Seriously? They didn't know you are a REALTOR®? Well them may have but perhaps you didn't explain that you can help out in other towns, cities and refer them to excellent agents in other states. People need to be trained on how you can help them; start the dialog and the conversations early. Tell your friends, family and those you meet that you are a licensed REALTOR® in the state of (fill in your state or states). However, you have contact in all 50 states you can refer them to!

How do I market myself? What is right for me? Think about what you already do. Are you an athlete and play on a team – let your team members know you are a REALTOR®! Are you a parent? Network with your children's parents and teachers. Do you buy coffee in the morning from the same place? Leave some business cards there! Network, phone calls, talk with agents, caravans, buyer counselling session ...ALL THINGS LEAD GENERATING.

Build Your Tribe

Your tribe is "THE LIST" not craigslist or Angie's list - but your money list. This is exclusively your list of businesses you use, know and trust to refer business to. This list is something you build over time, but be sure to keep this list handy. In order to be the "go-to" expert you want to be ...you must surround yourself with other experts.

Let your tribe know you are a REALTOR® and will be sending them referrals. Also let them know that you would appreciate them sending you any referrals for real estate. ALWAYS ask for the business. If they are not in need of your services now, ask them if they no anyone that is in need of a REALTOR® and if they will make the introduction, or at least give you their contact information.

This list should include the business name, contact name, phone, email and website.

☐ **Airports**: for your client who travel for business or have family from out of town ...know your local airports, where they are located, how people commute to and from them, times to avoid the area. Learn all about the international as well as the smaller airports.

☐ **Airport transport:** what is the best way to get to the airport? By car? By water taxi? Is there a commuter rail or a train that takes you there? Get to know how people in your areas travel.

☐ **Air purification systems**: depending on where the house is located, allergies of people who live in the home, you may want to purify the air. This is especially true in basements, which were actually designed for the house to breathe, not for people to be living, playing games, working out and relaxing in. An air purifier will remove harmful toxins and gases from the air. My favorite is the Dyson air purifier.

☐ **Beaches**: if you are in a coastal community know what beaches to go to; if there is public parking or beach stickers that can be purchased and if there is a snack bar and restrooms. If you are selling a home on the water, note when the high tide is and how far it comes up. Some homes will experience flooding in their yards and homes during high tides.

☐ **Builders**: who are the builders in your area? What scale of projects do they work on? Are they new construction builders? Do they specialize in remodeling? In affluent suburban towns we are seeing more and more small homes being knocked down and larger ones being built. Keep that in mind when working with your buyers and sellers - the house you are selling may not be what the buyer is after, it may be the land. Also find out what projects are the builders are working on? Maybe you can be their sales agent ...or keep them in mind when a client is looking for land to build....

☐ **Cable & Internet Companies**: As homes become more and more wired, consumers want SMART homes. Be sure to know what the best service is for the area you are selling in and have the contact information at the ready. You will need to have your buyers and sellers call these companies prior to the closing of the sale. Some local ones in the North East are Verizon, Comcast ...who are your local cable companies ...and what are their rates?

☐ **House Cleaners**: who can come on demand? Have a list of several cleaners at the ready. Think about industrial cleaners those who help in larger areas as well as the local cleaners who can pop in last minute to help when needed. Has your client or house cleaner been extra good to you? Consider giving them a Dyson vacuum to make their work easier!

☐ **Caretakers or Property Managers**: these people are definitely needed for any estate that you are working with or larger properties that require a staff of several professionals to maintain and upkeep the home. Additionally, caretakers are needed in resort areas where homes are only occupied for a small portion of the year.

☐ **Carpenters or Woodworkers**: skilled professional that do work on both in inner fine detail woodworking of the house as well as those that frame and structure the home.

☐ **Caterers**: have a list of your favorite caters at the ready. There sure will be a birthday or some celebration in the new home, so leaving a list of your preferred caterers will be a sweet gesture for the new homeowners. For open houses and broker tours, sometimes you can be your own caterer - head to BJs or Costco and order a platter of sandwiches, a bowl of fruit and a case of waters and sparkling beverages.

☐ **Chimney Sweepers**: in mountain homes with wood burning stoves, chimney sweepers are needed to keep the home safe.

☐ **Decor**: I try to live my best holistic lifestyle, VivaTerra has everything I need for client gifts, home staging, design and decor at great prices. What stores do you use to make your house extra special?

☐ **Electricians**: who can you call last minute? Who has teams available to do large scale remodel projects? Get to know several different specialist and licensed electricians!

☐ **Excavation Companies**: who can clear the land for you for additions, custom built homes or even if you need septic work done?

☐ **Farmers Markets**: this is a great place for your client to meet their neighbors, local vendors and feel like part of the community. Make a list of farmers markets, dates and times they are open in your town and the surrounding ones to share with your clients! This is good info for social media posts too!

☐ **Festivals**: Some areas have annual festivals so it is important to let the buyers know that the area gets crowded during those times. For instance, out by Brimfield – which is the largest outdoor flea market in the world (and a designer's dream). It gets super traffic-y and busy during those times ...better to let them know now then find out later. Or if your house is by a carnival, waterpark, ball park or ski resort ...information is powerful so let your clients know! They will value your honesty and be thankful that you were up front with them.

☐ **Florists**: Nothing freshens up a home like a vase of fresh cut flowers. They could be from your garden or flowering tree, or maybe you picked up a dozen roses at Trader Joes, or sprung for an elegant display from Winston's. People love flowers for your open houses....or as thank you gift! Flowers are that extra special something and are always a part of every luxury establishment I ever worked at or visited. No expense should be spared for flowers.

☐ **Furniture Stores**: where can they go to get new couches, or a pool table? You will want to know the big box stores and where they are located, as well as the consignment stores. I get all my eco-friendly furniture online at VivaTerra. Find out other places to source amazing pieces. People oftentimes have to rent while their homes are being remodeled and need to furnish the home top to bottom ...having a great relationship with your furniture store owners can help get you what you need on loan or for rent!

☐ **Gardeners**: Are there people you know who can maintain gardens? A local garden club? Maybe you can start one! Get together to share plants and clippings :)

☐ **Gift Shop**: Some agents give their clients a small thank you give...a local favorite by me is Rustic Marlin (www.rusticmarlin.com) . They make wooden signs that are perfect for indoor or outdoor use. A couple other favorite are Marshes, Fields & Hills (www.marshesfieldsandhills.com) for their hand towels and custom canvas pillows ...and the Green Koala (www.Greenkoala.net) for locally branded candles. Find some local artisans to share with your clients ...or even better collaborate on a project with them to make it an extra special gift!

☐ **Grocery stores**: Where is the nearest Whole Foods? Is there a co-op to purchase locally grown meats, fruits and vegetables? Is there a local dairy who delivers? What are some of the more popular and discount grocery stores in the area?

☐ **Gutter cleaners** - Make sure you have your gutters cleaned out before the wintertime. Especially if you live in an area with a lot of snow forecasted. Ice dams can form and cause major damage with water leaks, and a snowball effect of the water flow through the drainage system. Do not let this happen to you ...either climb a ladder and clear them yourself or be sure to hire a gutter cleaner!

☐ **Gyms, yoga & wellness studios** – Do you work out at a gym or with a private trainer? Think about doing some personal marketing and pop your business card up on the bulletin boards or community boards! Find out what hours these places are open and become familiar with the services they offer. Make sure you introduce yourself to your fitness instructor (if you have not already) and let them know you are starting out in real estate - if they know of anyone who needs help to call you. Share the love, refer them to your clients and ask for the favor to be returned!

☐ **Hair Salons:** you are their resource...especially if they are moving in from a new town, so know your area! Know who is good! How far out do they book appointments? What hours do they operate?

☐ **Handymen or Fix It People**: Join your local facebook forum to see who is out there to help. Most towns have one ...and if not, start it up yourself! Oh and surprisingly, often times you can fix things yourself with the help of a YouTube tutorial.

☐ **Hardware stores**: Whether it is the local hardware store, or your huge Lowe's or Home Depot, you are going to be frequently these places, so get to know them!

☐ **Home inspectors**: these guys can make or break your deal....so know your market. Some appraisers are very expressive and like to make a huge deal out of everything they find with the house, which can scare buyers away. It is important to have the names of a few honest and to the point home appraisers to help move the sale along. As around to see who other agents use.

☐ **Interior designers**: I worked on the Junior League of Boston's Showhouse committee for many years and learned that there is so much more to interior design than meets the eye. Sure, everyone has their own style, but finding the right balance, meeting the client's expectations and preserving the integrity of the home are what turns the home into a magical place to live.

☐ **Insurance brokers**: You will need to have an insurance binder prior to your buyer closing the sale, so have a few names on hand should they ask you. Types of insurance include: homeowners, property, flood, car, etc....

☐ **Junk removal**: Will they come to the house and remove it for you? What do they charge? Who can scrap metal? Who can remove large items like couches? No neighbor wants to see a couch left out for the trash to collect (and in most town they will not collect that type of an item)....so be kind be courteous and find out before you toss out! A national one that advertises on TV often, is www.1800gotjunk.com

☐ **Lumber companies:** There is usually a major home store in most markets, like a Home Depot or Lowe's, but check around to find local lumber companies. They may have more personalized service or a better selection of lumber than the big box stores have.

☐ **Outdoor Furniture Suppliers**: SUNZ, Wayfair.com, Home Goods there are so many great places to find outdoor furniture. Find out who delivers and what their costs are!

☐ **Painters**: Both interior and exterior. Who is reliable? Who has the team to get the job done properly? Check with your local chamber of commerce or put out a message on facebook for referrals.

☐ **Photographers**: Think outside the box here. Yes, there are the real estate photographers the drone photographers and videographers, but there is also the portrait photographers for the special family photos. Ask around and see who your favorites are. Whose photographs and whose style best fit your brand and image? Align yourself with them to be sure you have a consistent profile and marketing experience for your clients.

☐ **Places of worship**: we are not allowed to discriminate here so if you mention one place, be sure to mention or list all the different options for places of worship available in your towns.

☐ **Pool Companies**: those who install pools, remove pools and maintain and clean pools. You want to meet them all and have their info at the ready!

☐ **Restaurants**: People love to eat out! Get to know the fun places, the diners and dives that have delicious food at great prices, get to know the maitre d's at your fine dining establishments and always know where the beloved fast food places are.

☐ **Tile Installers:** need a quick update to a kitchen? Re-tile the backsplash!

☐ **Transportation:** where the public transportation is, Uber, Limo and Car service.

☐ **Tree companies:** storms can bring down trees in an instant. Have a couple of tree removal companies in your phone to give out when needed.

☐ **School Listings:** what schools are in the area. Are there specialties like Montessori, Private or Charter schools nearby?

☐ **Snow Removal:** does the home have a long driveway or is it on a road not maintained by the town? You will want to find this out so that you can line up someone to plow out the area during snowstorms.

☐ **Solar:** so many people are interested in energy conservation. I personally went with solar for my home and have been licensed in solar sales for over 5 years ...so send them my way and I can help! Email me at Susie.Gillis@NEMoves.com or visit www.SusieGillis.com.

☐ **Spas**: Where do you get your facials? Your nails done? Your massages, waxing, electrolysis and botox? These are great places for you to network! You have a captive audience with your therapist, so you may as well tell them you are a REALTOR® and would love to swap leads (send people their way and have them refer you). Some people do this naturally, but if this is new to you, get comfortable and confident practicing your pitch on these professionals!

☐ **Staging Companies**: a vacant house can be a challenge to sell…people want an idea of what it will look like when they live there …if you have a talent for staging and can do it yourself…by all means go for it! If not, find a local company that can help. Check out houzz for some staging companies in your area. I also love wayfair.com if I need to purchase something like pillows to dress up a space quickly and on the cheap …or my all-time favorite place for inspiration is Pinterest. See the awesome boards I have dreamed up at www.pinterest.com/susiegillis   For those of your in New England or New York check out Setting the Space. They are worth every penny and can turn any space into one in demand.

☐ **Stonemasons:** What is the first thing people see when they come to your house? The outside! Stonemasons can provide loads of value by hardscaping driveway spaces, creating different levels of gardens, etc. Their work can take an ordinary home to extraordinary.

☐ **Water filtration systems**: often times the water from the town or wells is not clean enough or has a chemical taste to it. The best ones I have found are Aquasana water filters . They produce different systems that generate great tasting water that helps soften my skin and keep my hair fresh.

This isn't a fill in the blank list. It certainly can be if you already have established relationships with these service providers. This list may take years to develop. However, you want to cultivate your relationships with them. Let them know they are your preferred provider and a member of your tribe. You value the work they do and hope that they value your contribution as a real estate agent.

You may have 10 other types of businesses to add to your tribe. The goal is to build up your reference list as you build your business. This isn't a quick list, these are trusted professionals who you have worked with and trust. Anyone can google electrician and et a list of 100 of them. But who are the ones who do superior work, show up on time and charge a fair rate? Those are the electricians I can count on and I want as part of my tribe!

Your tribe is your GOLD

Treat these people just like you want to be treated - like gold. Your tribe is a community of businesses, entrepreneurs, and small business owners who are the lifeblood of your community. Everyone knows about them, everyone uses them, and they have spent years building their good reputations. This is your chance to align yourself with those respected business, so treat them like gold!

If they refer someone to you, make sure you follow back up with them with a note of thanks!

"Hi Mark from the Bakery - thank you so much for referring you Aunt Mary to me! I am calling her tomorrow to set a time to meet and promise to help her out as best as I can! Thanks a million for thinking of me!" and sign your name.

Send a quick easy handwritten note card. Or text if you must. But close the loop. Let him know you got the lead, are thankful for it and are reaching out to her. Once you meet with Aunt Mary, or the lead - let that person know that they were referred to you and make that connection even stronger! Be a person of your word and give them your best!

By forming solid relationships with your tribe, you are building the value of your worth and that of your business and your reputation. Send them thank you notes, when they refer you business. Drop by, say hello and see what is new with their businesses. Think about doing a marketing campaign with a few of them and do it! Get a local facebook referral business going with your recommended professionals. Drop them off a pizza, or a fruit display, something to let them know you are thankful and appreciate their business. Have fun with this group and be sure that their information is at the top of your mind, as you will be for them!

Being an agent is like juggling 6 vases in the air while watering the garden, painting the house and talking to your client all at once! It is insane! There are so many moving parts and pieces and you are expected to make this all look effortless. You have to be on top of things and you have to be SUPER flexible to go with the flow, think on your feet, and have the resources at the ready to get the job done ...all with a smile!

Your tribe is the group that you can 100% count on a rely on. You trust their level of service and know that they will get the job done quickly, efficiently and for the right price. You know that they will be there for you and your clients and provide excellent results for them. Grow, build, nurture, thank and refer back to your tribe.

REAL ESTATE TERMS

The Art of the Deal: basic real estate terms.

Memorize these terms, use them in your conversations, read up on them and start talking like a real estate agent.

✓ Buyer: the person, people, trust or corporation that is purchasing real estate.

✓ Seller: the person, people, trust or corporation that is buying real estate (that has an accepted offer)

✓ Buyers agent: real estate agent representing the buyer and acting on their behalf.

✓ Seller's agent: real estate agent representing the seller.

✓ Buyers broker: brokerage who the buyers' agent is represented by and affiliated with.

✓ Sellers broker: brokerage what the buyers' agent is represented by and affiliated with.

✓ Buyers mortgage broker: mortgage broker who gathers financial information from the buyer and determines how much they are qualified for a mortgage, then sources the mortgage for their buyer.

✓ Buyers attorney: real estate attorney representing the buyer.

✓ Sellers attorney: real estate attorney representing the seller.

✓ Home inspector: a professional hired by the buyer to review and appraise the house prior to closing the sale (this is required by the bank lending the money for the mortgage).

✓ Bank or Mortgage Company: institution that holds the mortgage on your property in exchange for lending you the money to purchase real estate.

✓ List: this is the price the real estate is listed for (everything is negotiable so it is a list, rather than a fixed price).

✓ Offer: this the amount of money a buyer is willing to pay the seller for the purchase of real estate. This number is written up on an "offer letter" stating how much the buyer is willing to pay, when they are able to close the sale, how much they will finance and with what bank (unless it is a cash deal), the date of the inspection, the anticipated date of close.

✓ Accepted Offer: the amount the seller agrees to accept from the buyer for the purchase of real estate.

✓ Market: where real estate is purchased and sold.

Styles of Homes

As you show homes and start having listings of your own, knowing the style of home you are representing and giving as much detail as possible will help enhance your buyers experience. Broadening your real estate vocabulary with as many different styles of homes will help you better communicate with your buyers. Below is a list put together in alphabetical order from homestratosphere.com. Visit their website to see photos accompanying each style of home listed:

- Adobe revival (mostly found in the south west: AZ, NM)
- Beach house or cottage - oceanside homes
- Bungalow
- Cape Cod
- Colonial
- Contemporary (larger windows, streamlined)
- Contemporary Craftsman
- Country
- Craftsman
- English Cottage
- Farmhouse (beautiful front porches and adjacent barns)
- Federal Colonial
- Florida (this is a Mediterranean look with clay tiled roofs)
- French
- Georgian
- Greek Revival (the columns will help remind you of this style)
- Log (cabins and mountain homes)
- Mediterranean

- Mid-Century Modern

- Modern

- Mountain (wood, logs, stonework)

- Northwest

- Prairie (flat roof, horizontal lines)

- Ranch (usually one level, homes a broad and stretch out horizontally)

- Shingle

- Spanish (white stucco with clay tile roofs)

- Southern

- Southwest

- Traditional (see Traditional Home magazine)

- Tudor (think of brick, with brown lines over white stucco)

- Tuscan (blends with the landscape)

- Victorian (ornate homes with moldings and expert woodwork)

For a full list of 33 different style homes and photos, check out:
https://www.homestratosphere.com/home-architecture-styles/

Chapter Four

Marketing

MARKETING

"You're always with yourself,

so you might as well enjoy the company."

– Diane Von Furstenberg

How do I market myself?

If you haven't majored in Marketing or taken a few marketing classes, do not fret! Think about how you want to be perceived in the real estate world. This should be in alignment with your personality & lifestyle, but not to exclude aspirational. You are developing your personal brand. Do you want to drive a flashy car, wear expensive clothes and sell in high end markets, like the folks on Million Dollar Listing? Then you need to align yourself with that market. You may choose to work with rentals and do fast transactions in the rental market, be sure you are branding yourself that way so people know who to go to. I don't want a Twix when I am looking for a Godiva.

LOCATION: Where do you live? Where do you want to focus your real estate selling? Are you in an urban market? Are there particular parts of the city you cover? Maybe you are a luxury international seller, or specialist in equestrian properties. Whatever you decide is your area of focus get to know everything about it. Why do I need to know that you may be thinking? It is to help you from wasting time. Say your location is near a stadium. You do not want to have any open houses during game time. Traffic will be horrible and people will be at the stadium while you are sitting in an empty house. Get to know your location & its people.

SKILL SET: What sets you apart from all others? Do you rock the phones with cold calling? Can you gather a crowd to an event? Sell your house for the highest price in the quickest amount of time ...for the least amount of money.

SOCIAL ORGANIZATIONS: Are you a member of any clubs? Philanthropic organizations? Academic Achievement Associations?   Reconnect with them and get involved!

BUSINESS ASSOCIATIONS: National Association of REALTORs®, local Chamber of Commerce, Small Business Administration?

ALUMNI ASSOCIATIONS: Your high school, college, fraternity, etc. They all have alumni associations and if they do not, start one! Become more involved with these institutions that have shaped you into the person you are now!

"The map is not the territory"

- Albert Korzybski

Photo by David McBee from Pexels

Learn My Territory

Your territory is the area you have selected to focus on. This could be an entire town or two - maybe even a zip code within a large town- or you may have isolated it to one condo development that you like or live in (or not). Regardless this is a group of people - an identified target area - you will be spending your time marketing to, calling, having events for, etc...

You will notice when you drive around that you often see the same people's names in the same areas. Maybe it's the same roofing company, construction trucks, or the same REALTOR®s. These are the market makers. They are the leaders in the local business who are well known, trusted and get repeat business.   These agents get multiple listings consistently.   One of your goals should be to become one of these well known, trusted community real estate agents and advisors. It is because people see their names on the signs as they drive by combined with good service and trustworthiness that people start to get noticed, and they get traction. Top of mind. You want to be the first thing people think about when they think of real estate. It is free advertising once you have a listing, but you need to first get the listing.

Meet as many people as you can in your territory. Some agents wear their name tags all the time, it never comes off their jackets. Others will wear a more discreet REALTOR® pin on their coats.   Something identifying them as in the real estate business. Ever notice near election time how local politicians will go door to door introducing themselves? It is to get your attention and get your vote! As a real estate agent, you too need to get their attention and instead of a vote, you want their referral.

Learn everything you can about your territory. Who are the selectmen or politicians, what matters most to the people who live here? What are some town issues that they are dealing with?   Who runs the town? Are there elected officials? A Board of Selectmen? Find out who can help make this town a better place and help them do just that! Perhaps there is an active organization like the Elks, Kiwanis, Rotary Club, and other similar groups.   These are people who are organized and here to serve and better the towns that they live in. Consider becoming a part of one of those organizations, or joining the school board or even run for political office. Becoming involved in your community shows that you care and that you work well with others for the benefit of many others. It is in giving that we receive.

Become the Local Expert

"Pleasure in the job puts perfection in the work!"

- Aristotle

What is a local expert? Sometimes the local expert is the person who grew up in the town, knows it forwards and backwards and is now a REALTOR®. Or perhaps it is someone who really loves a particular town that they visit, studied in or vacationed in - that person may be a local expert. Concierges, bartenders, they often become local experts too! Basically, a local expert is someone who is very knowledgeable about the culture within a town and enthusiastic about it!   Yesterday, I took my nieces to Newport, RI for the day showing then around all the different neighborhoods, restaurants … the grand tour. I know where to park, what streets to avoid, where the best places to visit are, great beaches, scenic routes, celebrity houses etc.   While I am a Boston native - I am also a Newport expert! It is a city I am passionate about and have spent a lot of my time visiting.

Being the local expert, shows how you are different from the next person. There may be 100 real estate agents in your town; why would anyone choose you to be their real estate agent? There is no secret sauce here, you need to earn your street cred. One success leads to another.

Maybe you can leverage your previous work here? Network with those people who already know and trust you and ask for their referral of you. Or spend some time volunteering? This act brings together people from all parts of the community for the benefit of those in need. What better way to meet people than by sharing their mission of helping others? The easiest thing you can do is work your tribe. There is a mortgage broker friend I have who I can call for anything. He doesn't even live in my town or anywhere near me, but his network is so extensive whatever I need, I know Matt has a person for me. That is what makes you the local expert.

Leverage your knowledge pool

Know when to ask for help...and it may be several times each day. I know some days I was texting senior agents 10-20 times in an hour for help on how to negotiate my first offer. I felt like I was bothering them, but they assured me that it is their pleasure to help and shared what worked for them. Which I adopted as my own practice and got the deal! I know I am lucky to have such wonderful and kind people to work with and this is not the case in all offices. But that is why you need to carefully select who you want to work for and with. These are your people!

You belong to an office for a reason. That is your tribe and that is your team. If you need help, ask for it! And don't just ask one person...

There are often times your issue has come up and several ways of handling things, so ask around and then decide what feels best for YOU! How do you want to proceed?

You are just starting out as an agent, but the brokerage you have selected to work with has more than likely been around for a long time. Leverage all of that knowledge. Take advantage of it. This is by far the quickest way to ramp up in Real Estate. Align yourself with the people who have the answers. At the end of the day, it is your decision on how to proceed. And trust your instincts. If something doesn't feel right...or you feel awkward doing it...reconsider. Maybe the time is not right. However, it could also be your fear stirring up within you.

Your personal pitch

Your personal pitch is the first few statements you make when someone asks you what you do for a living as well as the answers to a few of the questions they most likely will be asking you.

In business, it is known as an elevator pitch. Something so short and concise, that it can explain to a stranger on an elevator ride, exactly what you or your business does. Write it, learn it, practice it in front of the mirror, take a video of yourself saying it and make sure it makes sense! Do not confuse people...keep it simple!

What do I do for a Living? I am a South Shore (pick your location) matchmaker! I bring buyers and sellers together in the real estate world (housing industry). I am a REALTOR®. I help people discover their dream home or sell their property. Make it sound like we are the professional, the experienced person ...this is the elevator pitch.

How's the Market? (Never say GREAT). If it is good for one, it is not good for the other. And right now, you do not know what side of the fence this person is on. Stay neutral. It depends on what you are looking to do...where do you like? Right now, in Cohasset things are really steady for sellers ...there is less than 2 months of inventory on hand. So, if you are looking to sell, you are in a great spot! Buy, sell, invest...what area are you looking in? Even the area will vary. Be honest, but do not lock yourself into one way of thinking. Listen more than you speak and work to understand what they are truly asking you.

You have no idea what angle this person is asking the question from so either clarify or go broad but truthful in your response. Remember you are Switzerland.

Pull market statistics, know the ratios of that town in the marketplace a couple of towns…. # homes on the market, average time on market. Pull up a couple of numbers before a party or networking event or even better, make it a daily or weekly practice:

- *How many houses are on the market in my town?*
- *How may have sold in the past 30, 60 and 90 days*
- *How many have been pulled or expired from the market*
- *Average selling price*

This is all good information that you can access through your MLS subscription under "Reports".

Be sure to know all the stats for my towns: population, who the board of selectmen, who is the harbor master, the chief of police, etc…

Keep a beginner's mind & stay open!

Perhaps you need to push your personal boundaries a bit and try something new. Try out a new way of doing things as clearly what you are doing now is not working. Allow yourself to be open enough to learn and experience.

Often times as adults, we think we have it all figured out. It may not even be that obvious that we think this way...and that is a blinder ...a shadow ...a part of yourself which you do not even see. A manager or a good mentor can help you see those blind spots, so that you can become familiar with them and be aware when they arise. Having this ability to self-reflect will help to make you all the better!

Each of you is coming into this profession with a unique skill set. That which makes you awesome, that which you have learned through the years and that has brought you success in other areas of your life. Perhaps you were successful in another sales job, or ran a household, or you have a magnetic personality which attracts people to you at parties and wherever you go! Or perhaps you are really smart and highly skilled at negotiating ...whatever it is that is your ace in your pocket - your natural skill set - leverage it!

However, in order to be prepared in any situation, you need to condition yourself to be comfortable in all situations. And notice when you slip out of your comfort zone. How do you feel? How do you react? You need to always play with a full deck, so start noticing what makes you uneasy and what you do not like doing and maybe try it out. Maybe you hate to cold call or hate to ask friends for help. Give it a try. Pushing through these self-imposed limits on our own terms will make it that much easier to manage when it is thrust upon us by a client.

"You can only become truly accomplished

at something you love.

Don't make money your goal.

Instead, pursue the things you love doing,

and then do them so well

that people can't take their eyes off you."

\- *Maya Angelou*

Personal Networks

This real estate career you are embarking on is all about marketing and networking. We live in such an amazingly interconnected world, whether we are social butterflies or wall flowers, each and every human being on this planet is part of some sort of network.

Work your networks! Talk to people, at the grocery store, at the post office, in your office (if you have another job) to your spouse or partner, to the parents of your kids' friends, your colleagues or people you volunteer with.

Begin to have active and constructive conversations letting each person you encounter. Let them know you are in real estate and would love to work with them. Ask for their referral should anyone they know need real estate expertise. That is IDEAL! Your golden ticket! When you have people out there recommending you and your real estate expertise, then you already have an advantage of someone else's approval rating. If that person already trusts them, then they will trust their referral. Make sure that referral is YOU!

Some people pay for lists. I haven't gone that route but I have done direct mail marketing to my network and to my neighborhood. If you pay for a list, make sure you work it to get your money's worth!

DIRECT MAIL: For direct mail campaigns, I pull a list from MLS within a certain radius of my home. I happen to live in a highly populated area, so I try to keep my list to about 250 people or half of a mile radius. Once I have my list, I always check to be sure to add "Or current resident". Some people rent their houses out or sometimes the database in not quite up to date, so you want to be sure that each piece you mail out gets delivered. All in all, because direct mail marketing is an out of pocket expense. It costs time to put it together and money for the printing and postal charges.

Notes: hand write them!

In the age of technology, nothing quite shows how much you care than a personal handwritten note or card. Especially when the norm nowadays is to shoot a quick text or an email. Hand writing a personal note means you went above and beyond to find the paper, pen or card, write out the note, find their mailing address, buy a stamp and send it in the mail. That shows that you are someone who will go the extra mile. Additionally, most people are now flooded with bills and junk mail, that receiving a well thought out card or letter is an absolute treat and break from the ordinary.

Pick 5-10 people a week to send a card to. It can be someone you have known forever, someone who you just met, your favorite waiter, bartender or your yoga instructor and write them a note. It also helps to track this information down somewhere in your company CRM (client relationship database), in an excel file or my mom's tried and true daily planner with everyone in her world's birthdays, anniversaries, retirements, work anniversaries...you get the picture. If it matters to you, write it down or have it somewhere easy for you to access. Facebook does a good job or reminding people, as well as google. I have so many people's birthdays on my google calendar that pop in automatically. Make the card heartfelt and meaningful.

This is a practice that was taught to me by my mother at a very young age. Taking the time to think about someone, and letting them know how you feel and that you care about them is one of life's precious gifts.

Offer to work the desk at your office

This is a great way to listen in on what is happening in your office as well as have a chance at getting some new business via telephone or a walk in.

Set aside a few hours each week to man the phones and sit at the front desk. It is a good way to learn who is who in your office, listen in on what deals are coming through and a great way to interface with the general public. And keep in mind be professional! I answer the phone *"thank you for calling Coldwell Banker, this is Susie speaking; how may I assist you?"*. Phone etiquette shows you are professional and well educated. Be polite at all times.

Working at the front desk also keeps your skills sharp because you will be entering info into Showingtime and reaching out to agents are information flows through the desk.

If your office allows up "up" time on the desk...jump at the chance if you can get it!

Network

Meet with industry professionals from complementary businesses

Many other businesses - like those in your tribe - who offer services that are complementary to real estate. For instance, in any real estate transaction you will need the services of:

- A real estate attorney
- An insurance company
- A mortgage company
- A title or septic company

Network with the agents and owners of these businesses so that they think of you when someone asks them for a great real estate agent!

In the case of attorneys, think outside the box and work with other types of attorneys, like estate or divorce attorneys. Often times these attorneys become the point of contact and decision for families and people dealing with divorce or death; two very uneasy situations to be in, and situations where most of the time an attorney is facilitating the divorce or executing the will. This means there is property to be divvied up or in most cases sold. You want to position yourself in the front of the mind of these attorneys so that if and when their clients need a REALTOR®, your name is the one that is given.

Websites

COMPANY WEBSITE: your brokerage may have a portal with sites on it for you. If not, here is a list of my favorite ones to use. Be sure to take advantage of your company website. With Coldwell Banker, mine is: https://susiegillis.cbintouch.com/

This is your way of interfacing with the public. It is basically a business card on steroids. On this site you can have:

- your contact information
- your message to the community
- a bio (a few paragraphs about YOU and your WHY or purpose for being a REALTOR®)
- your listings

COMPANY INTRANET

If you partner up with a larger brokerage, they most likely will have a company intranet. This is a website where all of your online tools, newsletters, office supply links, etc will be housed. It is your "command central" for managing your business.

MLS

The multiple listing service (MLS) is your gateway to the greater real estate marketplace. MLS is a must for every real estate agent. It is the golden gate for agents. This is where you launch your listings, share them and move them through the pipeline. This is where you see what is available for sale, what prices have changed, what houses have come off the market, when your open houses are, when the broker open houses are, as well as a plethora of other important information like property histories and tax data. This is your HUB of all real estate activity.

Zip Forms or Zip Logic

These are real estate form sites that allow you to create, authorize & distribute all your real estate forms online. Saves money on paper and ink and you can get your forms out to your clients faster. The best part is you can create templates, so whenever you have a new listing for instance, you can go in and all your forms that you need for the transaction are there for you to edit.

PERSONAL WEBSITE: www.SusieGillis.com

Personal websites are a great way to brand yourself and to tie together all your social media. You can highlight your listings on your website and give the public and idea of who you are as a real estate agent. I highly recommend that you purchase your own name and use it! This is a personal business, people buy from people they know, trust and love and while your brokerage may be well known, your neighbors and friends will think of your name first.

After all, your name is the brand you have for life! Brokerages or agencies come and go, but your name is forever. Your website can have other resources on it as you so choose like links to your "tribe" or preferred partners; links out to banks or lenders you do business with; community information and happenings. However personal you want to make it, it is yours!

NAR.REALTOR®

Search this site for up to the minute market statistics on housing from a national perspective.

Boost your salary and client base through continuing education and specialty training. NAR offers a wide selection of real estate training options for members and association executives, including classroom and online courses, training towards earning designations and certifications, webinars, and a Masters of Real Estate degree. As a member, you also have access to the world's largest real estate library.

Real Estate Update to the Community

You are a leader and a professional, now it's time to show that to the community! This is a great way to get people together, show your expertise & have the floor! Perhaps you live in a particular apartment building or development...start there and send out cards or have an open house at your home for your neighbors to come and meet you and hear about what you are doing in real estate and how you can help them. Is there a club house or common space in your building you can use to have an informational gathering?

Find a place where you can gather the community together. Maybe have a cocktail party, or lemonade one afternoon and invite them over to learn about what is new in the real estate market. Make sure that their time is well spent - add some value to them. Show them you know what you are talking about and have your statistics ready. How many homes sold in your area in the last 3 months, the last year. Did they sell for over asking, asking price? How long were they on the market for? What is the local employment rate? Is a new company moving to town and they are moving lots of their employees here too? Find out 5-10 interesting and unique statistics to your neighborhood to share with them.

Make it casual or formal...whatever most suits your audience and make it interesting. Let them know this is a briefing on the local real estate market and I will be asking for your help afterwards. Always ask for the business. Ask them if they know anyone who is looking to move into the area and if they would send an introduction to them for you.

Get the lead and make the connection quickly. A text or an email...or even a facebook friend request. Make sure you get the contact information for this person as they will become your client. Remember you are that local area's real estate expert. Ask too, if anyone is looking to sell their home? Take away the spotlight by saying "and if so contact me after this gathering to discuss – my cell is 508.xxx=xxxx And have handouts ready for them to take when they leave (do not hand these out before you talk or else they will not pay attention to you and will just read the note the whole time). On these handouts you must have the following:

✓ Your Name & Brokerage Firm

✓ Your Email - Your Website - Your Phone all in clear font and large enough for people to read.

✓ Your Photo – make sure it is a nice professional headshot of yourself looking your best and the most like yourself. Nothing is more confusing than a photo that has been retouched so many times you do not even recognize the person it is supposed to be. Natural is best.

✓ Key points of the presentation

✓ PIE CHART & Bar Graphs in COLOR

✓ Use a tag line...” your referral is my best compliment”

✓ Mail out the remainder of the handouts to those who did not attend.

✓ Place yard signs at each entrance the day of the meeting detailing location and time of the meeting.

This type of presentation can be done at a networking or BNI meeting, a non-profit you work with, you can present this at places of business and offices of referral partners, like at a local law firm or mortgage brokers office. There are endless ways of marketing yourself. Have your pitch down and have a 10-15-minute presentation always ready to go!

☐　　Have a guest list or check in list

☐　　Offer refreshments - water at the minimum with cups and napkins.

☐　　Introduce yourself clearly and concisely

☐　　Deliver your informal market update

☐   Allow neighbors to mingle and discuss

☐   Thank them for coming

☐   ASK THEM FOR THEIR BUSINESS - or their referral

☐   Pass out handouts of the key points when they leave

☐   Mail out handouts to those who did not attend or go door to door

Here is a quick script for a neighborhood meeting or can be used for networking:

"Hi I am Susie Gills with Coldwell Banker. Many of you I know and some of you are new faces ...so welcome and thank you for coming by this afternoon. This development (neighborhood, town, home, fill in the blank as needed) is my home. I have lived here for the past 10 years and it means the world to me. I take great pride in where I live and value the friendships, I have developed with you over the years. Some of you may know I am a REALTOR® with Coldwell Banker in Norwell, MA. Some of you may not know that already ...so I have invited you here tonight to share some information on our local real estate market."

Then present charts and graphs and have handouts ready for them with your logo on it. Keep the energy up and keep people engaged by asking the audience questions. For instance, who in this room was the first resident of this community? Let them talk amongst themselves...ask for stories, etc... Build a sense of community and use something they all hold near and dear to them - their homes - as the center of topic!

Direct marketing to the community

For those with a green thumb...or want to increase your exposure in the community try SEED PACKETS: I love this idea because if all goes well and they plant the seeds you give them.....every time they see that flower bloom they will think of you!

Make sure to have your name, photo, contact info, etc on this giveaway. Tape a business card to it.   These are great to leave by your front door for visitors who come by. Have them take a packet of seeds with them. Or perhaps the local library would let you leave a basket of them for the community ...there are so many ways to use this very easy marketing strategy.

At farmers markets – if you have a table at the farmers market or if they have a giveaway table, be sure to have your seeds there. These can be given to teachers for their students as well. Be creative and see how you can beautify your community while GROWING your business!

If you love to cook ...I have seen REALTOR®s make small jars of jelly or jam and write a catchy phrase on the outside of the jar. "To sweeten the deal". "Thank you for your business" or even the edgy "real estate is my jam". Whatever suits you.

Have pizza delivered to your new clients with "Thank You" written in pepperoni.

Raffles are a great way to gather information on your community. You can use either ballots or business cards whichever you think will work best and raffle off something you think a lot of people would like. Donate tickets to a professional sports game, popular concert, gala or event. Whatever you think your target market would be interested in. Maybe it is for an hour's worth of organizing or staging, or even cleaning services. I have seen scratch tickets raffled off, as well as food and gift baskets. Get creative and be sure to follow up with each person that entered! Most importantly make it (not necessary to be present to win).

Meet & Greet: host a meet & greet!

Time to get creative! Still looking for ways to stand out form your competition and meet more people. A meet and greet is an easy way to invite people into your office or home and do something fun! Keep real estate in the background and instead use the space to have fun!

☐　　Hand out swag bags with samples of local beauty products, or foods, or gift cards with your business card.

☐　Partner with another brand to foot the bill! In exchange, give them name recognition...” sponsored by...”

☐　　Have a raffle and pick a winner! Give out awards - a copy of Rock Your Rookie Year in Real Estate - (plaques, certificates, plant, gift certificate) to winners and make it so that winners have to be present!

☐　　　Make it fun! Have music playing, a guitarist, a band, or comedian.

☐　　Make it interactive, I once had 2 professional ballroom dancers come in and teach 15 of us for 2 hours...we ended up dancing for 6 hours and having the time of our lives!

☐　　Educate your audience! Invite an interesting speaker -- politician, police officer, contractor, celebrity.

☐　　Make the meeting a celebration of another successful year or of another "birthday" of the association -- the actual meeting becomes incidental to the festivity.

☐　　Feed them! Be sure to have food (wine & cheese, water, coffee & muffins, soda, snacks, sandwiches, catered meal).

☐　　Make a splash! With a pool party & barbecue.

☐   Keep them in the loop! Send out the save the date, the invite, maybe a teaser puzzle or game to do beforehand...get your crowd interactive and well notified of the event. Also try postcards, mailers, signs, emails, bulletin boards, etc...

☐   Invite the kids! And have the local high school kids be the babysitters!

☐   Showcase the new hotspots in town by having a meet and greet there.

☐   If needed and if alcohol is served, provide transportation to your office from a central area.

☐   Include an exciting topic of discussion (my area is FEMA & flood insurance).

Send thank you emails and follow up appropriately. Having the party at the office saves some money on renting space, and it never hurts to ask for donations from local food stores in exchange for your future business and referrals ...always keep your tribe in mind!

Social media

Take action! Real estate is an active profession; you need to constantly be alert and, on the move, to pick up new business....

Technology has significantly changed the way each of us does business. You can now shop online for a home and not even have to see it in person ...with drones and 3D technology you essentially can immerse your clients into the buying process from anywhere.

Having your social media up to the minute with relevant information is key!

My personal strategy is to keep content flowing through my channels. If the local Kiwanis is doing a movie night, that post goes up. If the garden club is having a sale or class, that post goes up. Anything that I feel is fun, or informative to my community goes through my instagram and facebook sites. The good thing is that others provide you with the content!

Then when your listings come in, people are already tuned into your channels.

INSTAGRAM

From a sales perspective, there are so many marketing avenues to take, so it is important you know how your target market (the people you want to sell for and to) communicate. Instagram...maybe you start an insta site just for your real estate ...or some of my favorites are the Nantucket sites which are operated by brokers, but highlight everything they love about their Island. Restaurants, science views, shops, events, etc...this is my personal favorite approach because it is not a hard sell. And it adds more value to me. I am more likely to view this page daily than if it is just homes for sale.

Use your hashtags! Hashtags are an online search method and help people direct towards their interests. People can run a search on a particular hashtag and your post will be included in that search. REALTOR® hashtags include:

#forsale   #realestate   #REALTOR®   #buyers

#sellers   #city   #brandnew   #MLS   #foreclosure

#buyerswanted #listwith(yourname)   #(yourstate)   #(yourtown)

#(yourneighborhood)   #newconstruction   #agent

#customhome #listwithsusie   #susiesells #seaside   #country

#southshore   #oceanfront   #cityviews   #urban #value #home

#homesweet #newhome   #victorian   #condo   #MLS

#investment   #citylife   #coastalliving #skihouse #scenichome

#property   #mustsee   #openhouse   #newtomarket#roofdeck

#hardwoodfloors #historichome #livehere #mansion   #pool

#landscape   #gameroom   #gardens   #waterfall

#seascape#oceanfront #community   #intown   #allseason

You get the idea! Don't overdo it with hashtags. I think 5-8 are enough, but some of my most successful social media artists use 10+ per posting; so be sure to include them in your postings to broaden your reach and following.

"In moviemaking,

you learn to pay attention to detail,

because so much is in the detail.

And when you're shooting,

you try to be very alert to what's going on,

even if you're tired."

- Frederick Wiseman

Online video content

Online streaming or video content educates the market. Showing these clips will give you street cred with your peers and build your real estate following. When doing these videos, think of the HG channel (Home and Garden) ...they capture viewer's attention for hours. So, pick a few things you like from a segment and video yourself offering these tips to your fan base. Take the time to do quick 30 second to 1-minute videos for youtube, instagram, and facebook teaching:

☐   tips on selling the home

☐   how to declutter: show before and after of a small room, drawer or closet

☐   how to stage a home for sale

☐   how to replace handles or pull on cabinets and doors

☐   mortgage info for buyers – have your favorite charismatic mortgage broker give a talk

☐   gardening tips: what plants are native, when to plant different vegetables, etc

☐   local festivals: music festivals, dance festivals

☐   large trade shows that come through the city

☐   local farmers markets

☐   school events: sports always excite and gather a crowd

☐   tours of parks: where the walking trails are, scenic roads, public beaches, etc.

☐   tours of historic landmarks

- ☐ local clubs and organizations

- ☐ status of the housing market

- ☐ local politicians: your mayor, city council or selectmen

- ☐ local celebrities

- ☐ favorite coffee shops: highlight the barista of the week!

- ☐ favorite markets

- ☐ favorite local candy stores

- ☐ best boutiques: clothing, gift stores, sporting, or art galleries

- ☐ colleges and Universities

- ☐ local breweries or vineyards

- ☐ local businesses or factories

- ☐ interview interesting residents of the town (with their permission of course)

- ☐ video the movie theatre on a Friday night

- ☐ Interview your tribe! Give them a moment in the spotlight and allow them to share their knowledge and expertise!

Something that is always of interest is to take footage of weather or a thunderstorm!

I like to capture the cloud formations as they cross the ocean. During one storm I posted my cloud footage on facebook and instgram. I wuickly received a message on Instagram from a meteorologist at the weather channel asking if they can use my video footage. I said abolsutely and he emailed over paperwork for me to sign off my rights (which I did not mind doing) in exchange for photo credit. Free advertising for me!

....that's another great way to build out your following! After signing off the waiver, they were free to use my video (you may even have been able to negotiate a fee in there, but I did it gratis).

☐   mortgage rate flashes

☐   new restaurants opening

☐   rare or interesting wildlife

☐   celebrity sightings

☐   goodwill or charitable endeavors

☐   promote a local fundraiser

"I have the simplest tastes.

I am always satisfied

with the best."

— Oscar Wilde

Best of your city/state/town list

For "Best of" Lists, we have Boston Magazine here in Boston which each August publishes a special edition of the magazine for the "Best Ofs" in the City. These are categories all voted on by the reader base....so maybe you want to try a local one of your own, and encourage your fan base to vote on their favorites.... then do a video on them! There is no shortage of footage in any town you live in....even if you are a REALTOR® in the middle of nowhere. Trust me, there is a market for people who want to watch grass grow...maybe time lapse it a bit; but they will watch it and it may even relax them!

The purpose of the best of list is to provide a resource to the community. Sure, there are google searches but with paid ads it is difficult to know what sources to trust. By having the readers or by having your local community members vote on who they feel is worth being THE BEST in their area of expertise, it is a true and fair honor. This also positions you are the trusted source for information, as you are bringing people together and giving them the options for the best foods and services in your town!

Who doesn't want to know what businesses offer the best in their town?

If your town does not already do this, get a panel of experts together and start your own! You can easily use survey monkey to create your survey of BEST OFs to send out to those who are interested or put a link on your webpage with when voting can take place for this honor. Let locals log in and put in their votes!

Make sure you have a deadline for the votes to come in and use your best PR skills to get media coverage! You want people to be excited about this reveal and to have interest in the event and who made the list!

Host a party or a special reveal event to showcase these fine businesses!

Below are some example categories to get your started on your "BEST OF" list:

Best Restaurant	Best REALTOR®	Best Diner
Best Hair Salon	Best Car Repair	Best Car Wash
Best Grocery Store	Best Landscaper	Best Bookstore
Best Interior Design Store	Best Pet Shop	Best Car Service
Best Boutique	Best Barber Shop	Best Cocktail
Best Night Club	Best Bakery	Best Bartender
Best Builder	Best Florist	Best Spa
Best Coffee	Best Pizza	Best Juice Bar
Best Personal Trainer	Best Café	Best Jeweler

FACEBOOK

Facebook in many instances can be your best friend. It is a very quick way to get the word out about your property and have greater exposure to your local network. Millions of people are logged in, tuned in and scrolling through facebook throughout the day it is often the best place to have the broadest reach (most people seeing your listing, info or ad) at the lowest cost.

Some REALTORS® setup a REALTOR® business page separate from their personal page and others just put their listings under their personal pages. I don't think the rules are et established for how real estate agents need to identify themselves on social media, but to err on the side of caution, have your name, photo, brokerage and contact info on each post. Real estate is a very personal business so either is fine as long as you are comfortable with it.

Photos - please make sure you have clear, interesting, exciting or meaningful photos. People love to look at pictures so use photos to highlight the best of your listing. They can be funny, or quirky, inspirational or informative - but having a photo will help so much more than just writing out text.

Announce open houses through facebook or schedule appointments with it. It is a quick way to spread the word. There are business profiles you can create and interact with your clients through facebook for events, open houses, listings, etc.

Look for larger groups on facebook to connect with - or start one of your own! Seattle rentals or Summer Rentals of Alton Bay, San Francisco Yard Sales. Be specific and be the group leader so you can control content and build out a large following.

SNAPCHAT

Millennials are all over this and they are the ones buying now...so consider snapping your listings!

As you move through different homes you tour, snap them out to your followers.

HOUZZ

This site is for professionals and a great place to go to build out your tribe! "When founders Adi and Alon remodeled their home, they started the way these projects often do: with a tall stack of magazines and referrals for home professionals from people they knew. But after those piles of torn out pages failed to make their dream a reality, they felt stuck. There had to be a better way.

So, they built Houzz. A place to browse and save beautiful home photos. A place to find the right design and construction professionals. A place to connect with others who have been there too. Houzz started as a side project but has become a community of more than 40 million homeowners, home design enthusiasts and home improvement professionals—across the country and around the world.

Whether you are starting a complete kitchen remodel or just looking for the perfect bedside table, the Houzz community of homeowners and professionals is here to help. And when you are ready to start your project, Houzz is the best way to get inspired, discover products and to find and collaborate with the perfect architect, designer or contractor". - www.houzz.com

HOOTSUITE or MASHABLE

AGGREGATE SOCIAL MEDIA apps are used to centralize your social media efforts. You create content in one place and the software then sends it out to all your handles (facebook, instagram, etc). This will save you time and money. Assuming you keep a consistent profile and have the same type of messaging for each outlet. Some people use different sites for different aspects of their businesses, so keep that in mind.

SOCIAL MEDIA QUICK GUIDE

For Realtors & Real Estate Agents

THINK BEFORE YOU POST

Before every post you send, think:

1) Will this be fun, useful, helpful or of value to my audience?

2) Is this in alignment / "on brand" with me & my local market?

3) hIs there a call to action to keep them in the loop?

	Frequency	Optimal Time	Photo Size
FB	1-2 a day	1-4 PM	1200 x1200
INST	1-2 a day	11-2 PM	1080 x 1080
PIN	1-2 a day	7-11 PM	736 x 1104
TWITTER	5-7 a day	12-4 PM	1024 x 1024

ANALYTICS TOOLS	GRAPHIC DESIGN TOOLS
Google Analytics	Instagram
Pinterest analytics	Illustrator
twitter analytics	Layout

AGGREGATE OR SCHEDULING TOOLS

	FB & TWITTER	PIN	INST
Wordpress	*	*	
Buffer.com	*	*	*
Hootsuite	*		*

POST IDEAS

New Listings	Coming Soon	Market trends	Just Sold
Local Events	School Closings	Weather	Design Tips
Staging Tips	Gardening Tips	Recipes	Kitchen Trends
Outdoor fun	Carnivals	Charity Events	Real Estate Quiz

Chapter Five

Get Organized!

"For every minute spent organizing,

an hour is earned."

- Benjamin Franklin

Get organized!

In real estate, you need to set up good systems right away to stay organized. There are so many parts to a transaction and often times you have several transactions going on at once, so find a way to maintain some order for your business. Additionally, unless you are in a hot market, you may find yourself working with the same clients for weeks or months on end...or if they are really particular could be years.

Some options for data recording include:

- If you are a paper person, get your file folders out and label them by street or address
- For my laptop people, create an excel spreadsheet with all the homes your toured and your remarks
- I use NOTES on my phone to list addresses, dates, who I met with, condition of property, etc
- Instagram – shout out on Instagram to see the house

If you are a paper person: Whatever your style is, do it and stick with it. Repetition is the key to success. Having things organized in the same place will make it so much easier for you to access your information when you need it.

Put together a binder

Most information is available online, so either find a way to virtually access the data you need or physically create a binder. I ended up putting together an actual binder which I keep in my car, because I figured if my phone died or I didn't have internet access, I can always pull a hard copy of a document that I need. In this binder I keep:

-        The copy of my real estate license

-        Nondisclosure agreements

-        Smart Phone

-        Blank Offer Letter

-        Blank Purchase & Sale Agreement

-        Business Cards for myself

-        List of my tribe: all those people I refer business to and who refer business back to me.

-        Open house signage

-        Open house facilitator sign (if you are covering someone else's listing)

-        Sign in sheets for open houses

-        A pen that works

Photo by energepic.com from Pexels

CARPE DIEM!

Day planner

The day planner is a tool to help keep yourself and your business accountable. REALTORS® are independent business owners, so it starts and ends with you. Creating a framework for your week will help keep your momentum going and discipline you to have the competitive advantage over the other agents. You can do this in google calendar, or you may prefer printing out or writing your calendar out on paper. Again, do what works best for you!

The day planner breaks up your week by tasks you want to accomplish.

Some of the most important segments include:

- ✓ Affirmations
- ✓ Call Block
- ✓ MLS
- ✓ Door Knock
- ✓ Drops
- ✓ Email Marketing
- ✓ Social Media
- ✓ Networking Groups
- ✓ Volunteering
- ✓ Open Houses
- ✓ Meetings
- ✓ Reading
- ✓ Fun

Yes, fun is on the list! Why work so hard if you cannot have some fun?

"You've gotta keep control

of your time,

and you can't

unless you say no.

You can't let people

set your agenda in life."

- Warren Buffet

Affirmations

Affirmations are the best way to keep your head in check. There can be a lot of discouraging moments in real estate, so you need to be able to pick yourself back up when it feels like nothing is coming together for you. Some of my favorite affirmations are: My business is growing every day. My clients love the work I do for them and pay me very well to do it. My bank account keeps growing! People love working with me and refer me to their friends and family. Each day I am getting better and better in every way.

Call Block

Set aside some time to rock the phones. Most people do not enjoy doing this but at least give it a try. An hour or more each day when you get on the phone and start making calls to let people know you are in real estate. If you are scared to make cold calls to people in the neighborhood find reasons to call them. Maybe a house just went up in the neighborhood, call around and introduce yourself as a REALTOR® and see if they know of anyone who is interested in living in this neighborhood. Some people call this their hour of power...others consider it dialing for dollars.. Either way it is the most important part of your business, MAKING YOURSELF KNOWN. Practice COLD CALLING.

MLS

Check the MLS to get to know your market. Log in and check the MLS each and every day. Several times a day if you can and see what is out there and what it costs. What new properties have come on? What new ones have sold? OR go for the gold and see what listings have expired and call around to the owners to see if you can scoop up a listing. Trust me, you want to know exactly where a property is and how much it costs when you run into someone in the grocery store who is looking to buy and knows you're an agent.

Door Knock

Get out and meet your neighbors! Check with your local laws to see if this is allowed...but some agents find it productive to go door to door and introduce themselves as their local REALTOR®. If it is not allowed, use the same practice but as you go out and about during your day.

Introduce yourself like you would be approaching someone's house to the people at the nail salon, gas station, the supermarket. Become more social!

Drops

Drops are a form of targeted marketing. For instance, stopping by at your tribe or local influencers (people who are prominent in the community...your doctor's offices, attorney's, town hall, etc) ...stop by and have something for them.

Perhaps you bake some cookies or bring some pastries along with a note of appreciation for the work they do along with your business card or a fact sheet about local real estate trends or mortgage data. Have something of value for them along with a treat!

Thank them for their service and ask for their referral!

Email marketing

Send out personal emails to friends, family, former coworkers, or purchase a list of names to reach out to. Have something creative or informative for them to read. Run a market activity report and show them how their neighborhood is doing for real estate sales. Keep your name out there and at the forefront of people's minds.

On major holidays you can create one really thoughtful email with a photo and send it out to your list to let them know you are thinking of them!

I feel that people are becoming more and more desensitized to email, but having a recurring one for major holidays or on their birthdays can be a nice way to keep you in their minds!

Social Media

Work your networks! People buy from people they love and people also buy from people they trust. What better way to launch your business than by helping a friend find their dream home!? Come up with a creative way to stay in touch. I have a special Facebook page for real estate and I share the things that I love about the towns I most frequently sell in. I also advise my network of properties that are "coming soon" so that excitement builds up and people are already thinking about going to your open house. Integrate your Instagram account with Facebook and all your other social media sites and have a clean and consistent message throughout your space.

Networking groups or BNIs

These are local groups of business professionals that meet weekly and share leads with one another. Some have pretty strict rules to follow in terms of meetings you must attend, leads you must provide and dues you must pay; and others are more loosely organized, so find one that best suits your style.

There is usually one professional from each field invited to participate. Or seek out your alumni associations, non-profits you are active with, your children's friends' parents, your parishioners...you name it let them know who you are and what you can do for them.

Volunteer

Give back to your community and meet people you may otherwise not have interfaced with. Giving back puts life into perspective and teaches us so much about ourselves and humanity.

Some people use their volunteer time to market themselves, their brand or the nonprofit they are supporting. Using photos of pictures of the good work they are doing to fill in their social media feeds. I have a different approach and prefer to volunteer strictly for the sake of helping others. Your style, your choice - just help!

Some national and popular charities include:

Habitat for Humanity www.habitat.org Habitat for Humanity is a global nonprofit housing organization working in local communities across all 50 states in the U.S. and in approximately 70 countries. Habitat's vision is of a world where everyone has a decent place to live.

Habitat works toward our vision by building strength, stability and self-reliance in partnership with families in need of decent and affordable housing. Habitat homeowners help build their own homes alongside volunteers and pay an affordable mortgage.

Toys for Tots www.toysfortots.org The basic mission of the Marine Toys for Tots Program is to collect new unwrapped toys and distribute those toys to less fortunate children at Christmas. The primary goal of

Marine Toys for Tots is, through the gift of a new toy, help bring the joy of Christmas and send a message of hope to America's less fortunate children.

Cell Phones for Soldiers https://www.cellphonesforsoldiers.com/ Cell Phones For Soldiers is a national nonprofit organization dedicated to providing cost-free communication services and emergency funding to active-duty military members and veterans.

USA.gov www.usa.gov Some National programs to help out with.

> Serve.gov - Sign up to volunteer and create projects. Tool kits are available to help develop your ideas into projects.

- PeaceCorps.gov - Volunteer abroad. Work within communities to improve education, health, the environment, and more.

- CitizenCorps.gov - Get training in first aid and emergency skills. Volunteer to support local emergency responders and disaster relief efforts.

- NationalService.gov - Offers grants for service and volunteering. Programs include the AmeriCorps, Senior Corps and Social Innovation Fund.

- Volunteer.gov - Volunteer in American's public lands, including our national parks.

- <u>Volunteer.VA.gov</u> - Volunteer at a Veterans Affairs (VA) facility in your area.

- <u>Federal Election Volunteers – Become a Poll Worker.</u> Help election officials in your state run the polling locations.

- <u>Earth Team Volunteers</u> - Work to improve soil and air quality on private lands. Conserve water and enhance wildlife habitat on private lands.

Open Houses

Volunteer to host open houses for other agents in your office if you do not have any listings of your own. Ask if you can shadow them. When you shadow an agent, you go along with them, but just to observe. You are not there to network and grow your business, you are there to learn.

Meetings

Every office should have meetings where information on sales, market trends, affiliations & closed business is presented, exchanged and discussed. My office has a meeting once a week for all agents and then other meetings are needed. Check with your office to see how everyone stays informed.

Reading

Set a goal to read one book per month - think of it as an investment in yourself. There are tons of real estate books out there, and my favorite self-help books to improve concentration, my health, etc. Check out my favorite reading list at: http://www.holistic-health-works.com/library.html

FUN

What is the point of all of this if you are not having FUN!? You have to schedule yourself for fun. After all, if you are not having fun, what is the point? I find that when I am the most stressed, things don't seem to go the way that I would like them to go. Having spent years studying mindfulness and a yogic approach to life, I discovered the importance of taking a step back and "lightening up" as my father would say. Dig deep, do the work, but find a way to have fun through this process! When you enjoy the work you do, you will never "work" another day in your life.

Learning

Continuing education because there is always something new to learn! Look for local classes to sharpen your skills. Does your office offer continued education? I know Coldwell Banker has hundreds of classes online and in person to attend. If your office does not offer classes check with your local REALTOR® board. They have classes on ethics, leadership and all other real estate related classes that can help you as you evolve in your real estate career. If you want to speak better in front of others, consider taking a Toastmasters class or one of Earl Nightingale's classes.

These are all examples of things that need to be done in a day. Do you need to do them all? That is totally tour call. I will suggest trying them all out and seeing where your time is best spent, and it is not always doing the fun things. Often times, the rewards and commissions come from doing things that are not easy for us, or that we do not like to do.

Give it a try!

"Don't be fooled by the calendar.

There are only as many days in the year

as you make use of.

One man gets only a week's value out of a year

while another man gets

a full year's value out of a week."

-Charles Richards

Calendar sample

Real Estate moves fast and your days will more than likely never go according to plan; however, having a framework or calendar in place at least at the start of your career will help keep you focused and on track. The most important thing you should be doing is trying out what works for you. This job can be done a million different ways. Here are some tools and guidelines that successful agents use to stay on top of their best game.

Keep daily activities and making small gradual progress with:

- Call blocks
- Follow up activities
- Prospecting for new appointments
- Marketing Campaigns
- Call arounds to neighbors of new listings

The chart following is a framework for you to consider. Try it out for a week and see if it helps. Maybe you need to allocate more time to a certain activity, then do that. Adjust it to fit your needs, but by all means stick to the program.

Maybe you can be more focused by having a set schedule. Working with a framework, you can have something to strive for, but there will always be changes in your schedule. You will get called out to help with an open house, or you will have a client wants to see a property during your call blitz. Just be sure to get that task done that you skipped in the next day or two.

You don't have to stick to it 100% every day, but be sure to get all the tasks done within the week. Consistency is the key to any success. With a touch of focus you are a star!

	Mon	Tue	Wed	Thurs	Fri	Sat	Sun
6-7	DAY		READ, AFFIRMATIONS, MEDITATE				
7-8		CHECK THE MLS: rentals, new to market, surrounding towns					
8-9	OFF	Office	Shadow		Mailings or	Showing	OFF
9-10		Meeting	a Senior	TRAINING	Marketing		
10-11			Agent		Free	TOUR	Prepare for
11-12		TOUR		Volunteer	Time		Open House
12-1			LUNCH: bring clients or referral				

		partners					
1-2		DI AL FOR DOLLARS					Open House
2-3	UP DESK	SO CIAL MEDIA: work your networks!					
3-4		Follow Up	Meet w	Volunte er		OFF	Close up OH
4-5		with Clients	your manag er	Showi ng			
5-6							
6-7							
7-8		CHECK THE MLS					

"Be accountable for your time and respectful of others'".

-Susie Gillis

Punctuality

Be there on time. It's that simple.

If it is not easy for you to be on time, then plan ahead. Make sure you have coverage at your job, or for your kids, check WAZE or another driving app to see how long it will take you to get there in current traffic conditions, account for the time it will take you to find parking, or to maneuver a parking garage and walk to your appointment, make sure you have eaten. All those things we learned getting you to the real estate exam apply here and every time you have a meeting or appointment to be at. That was your training, now this is showtime!

Whatever you have committed to do, be sure you are there on time and ready to focus. How do you feel when you take time off to go to a doctor's appointment and the doctor is running late? It is annoying right? Do not be late for your clients or prospects because you may not get a second chance with them.

If it is a listing appointment, often times the sellers have set up a whole slotted schedule of other REALTOR®s, so if you are late, you will miss your chance. Being on time says you care and that this is important to you. It shows your professionalism and that you value the other person's time.

The other side of this is that most people in the world are not punctual. They could care less about another person's time and are often if not always late. You need to forgive them and be patient, but never let yourself be one of them. If this is how another agent you are competing for business against operates...guess who naturally will have the advantage? The person who shows up on time and is reliable.

If this however is a client or prospect who continually is not reliable to be on time, then you should think about whether you even want to work with a person like this. If they are like this for a first meeting, this behavior may carry on throughout your entire time working with them. So weigh it out. It may be worth it to you, or the stress of not being able to count on them may be too much. Your call.

Lesson learned: always be on time for an appointment. And when managing contracts, always have a date and time due on them to prevent parties getting agitated. As a REALTOR®, you are an intermediary. Your patience and tolerance levels are different from each of the parties you are working with.

Time management skills

"Nothing is a waste of time

if you use the experience wisely."

-Rodin

Make Your List of Priorities.

What are your priorities? Simply put they are all the things you either want to get done or have to get done. The key in being most productive is taking a close look into what your priorities are and then seeing what ones are most crucial to your livelihood and success. What is most important to you? Is it you yourself? Your family or loved ones? Is it making money? Do you like helping others? Write down all the things that are a priority in your life. Then rank them from most important to least important.

Set deadlines for these tasks and stick to them. Is it something that needs to be done this minute, within the day, week, month, year; write down your delivery date for each action item (things you want to accomplish)? If you need help with some software, use your google calendar or for more complex workflow management use software like Asana which allows you to track and assign tasks to others on your team.

☐ If it is important, write it down in your phone, notebook, somewhere you can find it.

☐ FOCUS ON WHAT IS MOST IMPORTANT FIRST.

☐ Break down your goal into smaller steps.

☐ Brainstorm all possible ways to approach or solve the task at hand.

☐ Can I rely on outsourcing to help?

☐ Is it cheaper to pay someone to do this or to do it myself?

☐ Take deeps breaths and be mindful of what you are doing. Focus.

☐ Use music or photos to inspire you!

☐ Shut your phone off if you need to stay on task.

Priorities are what matter most to you. Sometimes we have several priorities in which case we need to choose what is most important and what can wait until after this most pressing issue is taken care of.

Your priorities are what fluctuate throughout the day, so have a list of them will keep you on track. I recall a coworker of mine kept a copy of his mortgage bill at his desk to remind him why he was at work. To keep himself focused on producing the income he needed to support his family. While this may be a little too stressful for some people, he needed to see exactly why he was working so hard!

My Top Priorities are:

_____

_____

_____

_____

_____

_____

_____

_____

_____

_____

_____

_____

_____

_____

_____

_____

Why are these my top priorities?

_____

_____

_____

_____

_____

_____

_____

_____

What will happen if I do not take care of my priorities?

_____

_____

_____

_____

_____

_____

How will I feel when I have taken care of all of my priorities?

_____

_____

_____

_____

_____

_____

_____

_____

_____

_____

_____

_____

_____

"This is the beginning of a new day.

God has given me this day to use as I will.

I can waste it or use it for good.

What I do today is important, because

I am exchanging a day of my life for it.

When tomorrow comes,

this day will be gone forever,

leaving in its place something

that I have traded for it.

I want it to be gain, not loss;

good not evil; success not failure;

in order that I shall not regret

the price I paid for it."

\-   Author Unknown

Chapter Six

Financials

"Money is only a tool.

It will take you wherever you wish,

but it will not replace you as the driver".

- Ayn Rand

Financials

Financial Needs & Goals

It is true, real estate agents (for the majority) work strictly off commission. Therefore, it is important that you know your finances and budget for the year ahead of time. It is often said that it can take a year or more for a REALTOR® to get their first paycheck. If you are reading this book, it is highly likely that you will absolutely NOT be part of that statistic. But I want to be sure you are covered all the same.

Now I certainly hope you have wild success from the start and have millions of dollars in closed sales within your first few months, it is rare that that success occurs. So, you need to plan ahead!

It takes a lot of stress out of the job by giving yourself the financial cushion to launch your career. You certainly do not have to have this in place to get started, but it certainly helps!

Your goals can be financial, personal development, "what do I want to improve on", or maybe you want to buy a house of your own. Take some time to think about what your financial goals are. Maybe you have tuition to pay for yourself or your children, would like a new car, or a mountain home.

Give yourself the space to dream up the life you want to live and them go about creating it for yourself!

"The only limit to the height of your achievements

is the reach of your dreams

and your willingness to work for them."

- Michelle Obama

Budget

Your real estate commissions (your earnings) are a direct result of your sales as you are 100% commissioned agent. In order to come up with your annual sales goal; first we will need to pull together your current expenses and work our way back. But before that, look at all your current living expenses, debts and dreams and itemize each one of them.

This can be a very uncomfortable exercise for some people, but it will feel so good afterwards and put you in a position of financial power. You will know and be fully aware of exactly how you are spending all your hard-earned money. Rip it off like a Band-Aid, and gather all those financial documents, bills, account statements, tax returns, etc and begin to put it all together.

Breathe.

Pull up all of your billing statements, debit, checking and savings account records, tax returns and start combing through all of them. How much money do you actually spend?   The basics and the priorities should always be food and shelter (see Maslow's Hierarchy of Needs from https://www.simplypsychology.org/maslow.html) - so all your costs for groceries and restaurants and then your rent or mortgage payments. Those need to be paid first.

After that look over where all your money is going, add it up by category and write it down in the chart below.

Photo credit: https://www.simplypsychology.org/maslow.html

In order to reach the higher levels of living a self-actualized life, you need to start from the bottom up. Just like you build a home from the ground up, you are building the life of your dreams from the ground up!

Now let's get back to the basics and see where all of your money is going.

The following is a spreadsheet and guideline for you to use to track all your personal expenses. Print it out, fill it out and be honest as you are doing this. The topic of finances can be very intimidating for many people, but it DOES NOT have to be. By taking positive steps in the right direction you can be financially independent and secure in the future!

Make a spreadsheet (to stay organized) and on track:

PERSONAL FINANCIAL STATEMENT

Rent or Mortgage Payment $ _____

Real Estate Taxes $ _____

Solar and/or Electricity $ _____

Gas or Oil Heat $ _____

Car Payment / Uber / Public Transportation /Gas $_____

Car Insurance $ _____

Grocery Bills $ _____

Gym Membership $ _____

Clothing / Household Allowance $ _____

Cell Phone / Cable / Internet $ _____

Credit Card Debt $ _____

Dues or Fees $ _____

Tuition $ _____

Child care $ _____

Travel Expense $ _____

Spending Money $ _____

Investments $ _____

Savings $ _____

= TOTAL_____

Add all of this up and this is what your monthly living expenses are (the TOTAL). This varies person to person. But now you know what it costs you to live each month. If the number is zero, put that 0 in there (and LUCKY YOU). Congratulations, you are already saving $$$.

Ok so now that you know how much it costs you to live each month, ideally you will have 6-12 months of living expenses saved up. Financial planners always suggest having an emergency fund of 8-12 months living expenses tucked away for a rainy day. However, you are now a REALTOR®, so unless you start producing and closing business on day 1, you need to have your living expenses covered for 6 months to a year while you ramp up and get your business started.

Let's do the math:

MONTHLY LIVING COST x 12 = MONEY YOU SHOULD SAVE UP

PRIOR TO GOING INTO REAL ESTATE

Now plenty of people work part time, or have other jobs while ramping up in real estate so this is not the cold hard truth, but rather a guideline for those without a net. Stress can wreak havoc on your body and mind, so by having the reserves set aside so you can concentrate on your business and not on your living expenses frees up a lot of mind power and energy you can direct towards your successful career as a REALTOR®.

By creating this list of living expenses, you can also see where your money is being spent. Are you spending way too much on your house costs and need a roommate or someone to share expenses with? Or perhaps you need to sell your home and move to a different location if your rent or mortgage is too high for you.

Maybe you are spending too much on your phone bill or cable. Are there channels you are paying for that you do not use or need? IS there a promotion to save additional money on your bill? Can you drop live TV all together and stream your programming? Is there a better deal being offered by another company?

Call up your phone and cable companies and see how you can lower your bills! Let them know that the competition has a better offer and while you would like to stay with your company, you will have to leave if they cannot at least match their competitor's pricing. Practice your negotiating with them and remember when you use your closing question...then...REMAIN QUIET.

The first person to speak loses.

"Setting goals is the first step

in turning the

invisible into the visible."

– Tony Robbins

So how much will I make?

First off, it is highly likely you will not make as much as you may think you will. And I will explain why that is so. When you see homes listed with a 3%, 4%, 5%, 6%, 7% whatever the commission is ...that is not the amount of money you will make on the deal. In most cases (unless you have both the buy side and the sell side) you will divide that number by 4. Each transaction has two sides – the buyer's side and the seller's side; the buyer's agent and brokerage and the seller's agent and brokerage.

For easy math, let's use 6% as an example of what the commission rate is that the seller has agreed to. Keep in mind this number varies, but is used here only as an example. So, with 2 sides, the buyers and the seller's sides, this is where the first split comes in – half to the buyer's side and half the commission to the seller's side. The 3% to the buyers and 3% to the seller's side. Now...it gets split again. Yikes! Yup, that 3% is NOT ALL YOURS.....(unless you have both the buy side and the sell side).....it now get split again between you and the brokerage office you work for...this too can vary firm to firm but in this example I will use half or 50% ....making your piece of the pie 1.5%. I know now ideal for all the work you will be doing!

So, for a $300,000 home here is the commission split math:

$300,000 x .06 = $18,000

$18,000 / 2 = $9,000 ($9,000 to the buy side and $9,000 to the sell side)

$9,000 / 2 = $4,500 ($4,500 is your piece of the pie)

HOWEVER

You need to hold aside taxes for the government and pay for your own health insurance.....so get selling! So that $4,500 quickly looks like with an example 25% taxes. $3,375 and then your health insurance and living expenses....you see how it goes. This is a numbers game...the more people you talk to, calls you make, and actual encounters with active buyers and sellers in the marketplace that more money you will make!

Earnings.....show me the money!

Safety

"Don't you dare underestimate

the power

of your own instinct."

- Barbara Corcoran

I like to keep a positive mind frame; however, it is never one of naiveté. There are potential dangers with being a REALTOR® so go about your work with caution ...and take every precaution you can. The goal is to always remain safe, by working smartly and keeping yourself on alert.

Try to have another person with you on your open houses. If you work in teams, your personal safety is increased and you will have another set of eyes helping you prevent things like theft.

Never go down the basement with people who are touring. Direct them to the basement and let them tour it at their leisure. They can always make an appointment with you or their agent if they want to go through the details.

If permissible by law, you may want to consider carrying mace. You never know when you will need to defend yourself. And on that note....

TAKE A SELF DEFENSE COURSE. The goal is to never need to use what you learn...but should you be in a precarious situation or a dangerous one....you will have the self-defense skills to get yourself out of there before you are hurt. Yell, scream, kick, poke their eyes out...whatever you need to do to keep yourself safe.

Knowing that you are safe and have the skills to defend yourself does wonders for your self-esteem too. Your confidence gets a boost! I spent a year studying MMA: Muay Thai and Jiu Jitsu under some of the best trainers! It was so uncomfortable for me, I laughed through my first several weeks because I was so scared. It was a nervous reaction to being so out of my element.

However, I began to crave my time on the mat. While I hope to never have to use these skills, it sure makes me feel a little bit safer knowing that I have some preparation.

When you are showing a house or conducting an open house, always, always, always text a spouse, friend, someone of your whereabouts. Let them know the name of the person you are meeting with, a photo if you have one, the time you are meeting and where you are meeting.

I always say the time I will be done and if they do not hear from me by that time, to send someone over! Be sure to text them when you are through, so they don't come looking for you. (This rule also works with dating.) It is better to be safe than sorry.

Chapter Seven

Working with Buyers

Working with Buyers & Sellers

It is an art working with your buyers and sellers, and starting out, you will definitely want to write most things down so you can remember what you discussed later.

Below is a sheet I use to gather information on my potential clients. Sometimes I fill this form out in front of them, other times, I fill it out right after I met with them and then information will still fresh in my mind.

Either way, get in the habit of tracking information about your clients down.

Tracking lead information

CLIENT INFORMATION FORM

Date: _____

Name: _____

Name 2: (Spouse/ Partner, etc):

_____

Property Address:

_____

City: _____ State: _____

Zip Code: _____

Phone Number: _____

Cell Number: _____

Phone 2: _____

Cell 2: _____

Work Phone: _____

Work 2: _____

Email: _____ Email 2:

_____

Family (names, ages?): _____

Pets?: _____

Have you spoken with other agents? YES NO

Are you working exclusively with an agent? If so, their name?
_____

Have you considered selling your house on your own? Yes / No

Why are you moving? Job, school, downsize, upgrade

What is your timeline?
_____

Do you know where are you moving to?
_____

What is the date you would like to be moved out by?
_____

Is that a firm deadline? Are these milestones you need to hit – start of school, new job, etc?

What are you excited about in the move?
_____

What makes you want to stay here?
_____

How eager are you to move? It is a must or a desire – like you want a nicer home.

_____

_____

When did you purchase your home?
_____

Why did you choose this home?

_____

What was the purchase price?

_____

What have you done to improve the home since you moved in?

_____

_____

What improvements?

_____

How much of a mortgage do you owe?

_____

Do you have an idea of what your home is valued at?

_____

Do you have a number you would like to receive for your home?

_____

Is there a bottom value – an absolute cut off of what you will not accept in price?

_____

Do you have any friends or family interested in purchasing your home?

_____

If so, what are their names and may I contact them?

_____

Are you open to that happening? Yes / No

How many bedrooms? _____

Bathrooms: _____

Square footage of the home? _____

Schools? _____

Favorite things you love about your home?

_____

_____

_____

_____

What do people compliment your home on?

_____

_____

_____

_____

How did you hear about me?

_____

_____

_____

Is there any reason you would not do business with me?

_____

_____

Next steps: from here I would love to come out and take a look at your home to get a better understanding of the neighborhood, and what I may be able to help you with. From there I will put together a market analysis and together we can decide what we think this home should sell for and how I can market the property for you! Is 2pm today good for you? Confirm the appoint, do some research on the area and the house, and be on time for your meeting!

WORKING WITH BUYERS

As a real estate agent, you can work with both sellers and buyers. The process is totally different with each one, so I will break it out in parts. So, you have a lead. Either you lucked out and they called into your office letting you know they want to purchase a house. Or maybe someone in your family or a close friend wants to buy a home and they have called you. Congratulations. You now have your work cut out for you and you need to earn their business.

Discovery phase

This is the first part of selling. When people are starting to think about buying a home or selling their home. Get an idea of the type of property your buyers are looking for (and keep your ears open when touring to hear of any coming on the market).

Be aware if they are asking discovery questions like:

☐   When was the house built?

☐   How many bedrooms?

☐   What kind of heat is it gas or oil?

☐   Is there a washer dryer?

☐   Is there a pool?

☐   When was the roof updated?

☐   When was the electrical updated?

These are all discovery questions asked at the beginning of a sales cycle. These are the fundamental questions (which are all answered on a well written MLS listing) that you can share with your clients. This means they are interested and want to know more about the property ...this is phase one of the buy cycles.

Find motivated sellers for your buyers :)

Your heave searched and searched the MLS for the perfect home for your buyers, but still nothing has come up that fits their needs. These techniques also work when you are looking for new listings and asking yourself where can I find new business? This is always at the top of a real estate agents' minds. You have exhausted your efforts with all the MLS listings to source your buyers' new home to no avail. Now, you will need to be open to finding them in unexpected places - so get creative!

1) The listing will indicate a call by indicating "motivated seller" or "bring all offers".

2) If you hear or discover that the owner got a new job and needs to move or for some reason needs to relocate.

3) If you notice that the house has been vacant, or is overgrown or not cared for.

4) If the mail outside of the desired home is piling out outside of the home.

5) If the family has another child or a family member moves in with them; they will outgrow the space and need to move.

6) Conversely, when empty nesters find themselves in a house much larger than their needs.... you have a motivated seller.

7) The home owners health is failing or they are elderly and in need of a different housing arrangement or configuration - sometimes assisted living; they often times will sell their homes.

8) When the property is listed as an estate property.... or better yet there is an estate sale....go for that listing!

9) Ask around to friends, family, other agents, your dentist, hairdresser - see is they know of a property that may be a great fit!

10) Check craigslist, facebook town groups, and signage for "For Sale By Owner" signs.

Recruiting sellers & buyers at an open house

If you are hosting an open house, you have two jobs:

1) to sell the house you have open and

2) to find new buyers who are not represented by an agent.

The first thing you want to find out is are they working with an agent? Immediately after you have greeted them and had them sign in - and remember to always, always have buyers sign in to the guest log or an open house app to track the feedback and the traffic of the open house. Right after they sign in, after that business has been cleared you should ask them "are you working with an agent"?

If they have their agent with them or they say yes, then you are pretty much hands off and allow them to tour the home at their leisure

...offering bits of information here and there. But their agent for the most part will want to control their tour and will only ask you questions when they need to.

If they are not working with an agent, then you want to put your best foot forward to learn as much as you can about them. Some of the questions I keep in mind are:

☐　 What are your names? (and do you best to repeat their names when addressing them).

☐　 Are you new to the area?

☐　 What brings you to the open house today?

☐　 Have you been looking at homes for a while?

☐　 What is your time frame to move?

☐　 What type of home are you looking for?

☐　 Do you have a home to sell now? (is no, move ahead) if yes – go for the listing (talk track below)

☐　 Are schools important?

☐　 What is your budget?

☐　 Do you commute to work?

Would it be ok if I sent you some listings based upon when you have told me you are looking for?

Now, you do not want to pepper them with questions, but rather casually through their time there find out as much as you can without making them feel uncomfortable. You are there at their service to help, so ask away!

Stay Customer Focused

You work exclusively for your clients. If you did not have any clients, well then you wouldn't be working, right? So, treat them like gold. Give them the time, attention and respect you would want.

It is important to figure out your client's expectations as early on as possible. Some as just casually looking so it is easy to overlook what they expect from you. Just because they are six months out from buying doesn't mean that they don't want to get out and see properties with you every week. Find out what their needs are, and be sure you can fulfill those. If you can't, decline the offer to work with them, or find someone to help you work with them.

Ask them questions like:

How do you want me to work with you?

Do you want me to send you listings daily?

Do you prefer that I call you each day, or text?

How often do you want to look at properties?

Do you prefer reaching out to me when you are r

"Before you speak, listen.

Before you write, think.

Before you spend, earn.

Before you invest, investigate.

Before you criticize, wait.

Before you pray, forgive.

Before you quit, try.

Before you retire, save.

Before you die, give."

-William A. Ward

Outlook with Clients

Be Switzerland! What does that mean? Keep a positive neutral ground. Remember when I said in your intro never to tell them if the market is good or bad? That is true. You do not know enough to make a one-sided opinion, so stay in the middle.

That being said, you always have to be yourself. Be confident & happy to have their business, but smart and aware of all the pitfalls that could occur. This is not your first rodeo (and if it is, please leverage your mentor). After all it is your skills, your personality, reputation or your name that got you the opportunity, now don't mess it up!

BE SWITZERLAND! Your opinion doesn't really matter. That might be difficult to hear, but your lens is not your buyers' lens. You have different viewpoint and unless asked by the buyer, keep your opinions to yourself. Listen and really look to understand what your clients are saying. If you start talking and saying what you think.... that can kill the deal right there.

 Don't yuck their yum! Just because you like mansions doesn't mean your clients do.... a cabin in the woods may be a better fit!

I find that the clients that want your opinion or at least say that you are the boss or 100% the advice they are relying on, they will still waver, fester and ultimately make their own decision. So best to stay even and neutral, always prepared and informed ...like Switzerland!

Never judge a book by its cover

I learned this lesson as a child from my grandfather. He was a successful entrepreneur who always taught me to treat EVERYBODY the way I would want to be treated. Be kind to them, and always make them feel welcome. No one is better than anyone else, he would say...especially on account of their financial situation.

When I managed a luxury boutique with all commission sales people, I noticed some salespeople would cherry pick (look for the well-dressed people who were affluent looking) who they wanted to work with instead of staying in the sales rotation. The rotation was a system where one sales person would get one person who walked in, the next salesperson, the next person that walked in, and so forth.

One day, a woman walked in wearing her sweat suit with no makeup on.... she clearly was running errands and getting a lot done. However, the usually eager sales people were nowhere to be found. Sure, they were all available but none of them wanted to waste their turn on this person who appeared to not be a fit for the boutique.

Nobody jumped to assist this woman, so as the store's manager, I helped her. It turned out she was a local socialite who was chairing a gala that evening and purchased $8,600 worth of items from me.

The sales associates were aghast when they saw the items she was purchasing and sulking in a way over my good fortune. After she left, I reminded them never to judge a person by what he or she is wearing or looks like. You never know who you are working with, so treat everyone with kindness and respect you want to be treated with.....isn't that the Golden Rule?

In real estate it is even more important. In the book The Millionaire Next Door by Thomas J. Stanley and William D. Danko, the millionaires are those who work hard, live modestly, have most if not all of their assets already paid for and save their money. They are not always the ones driving the Ferraris living in massive estates.

These millionaires are smart with their money, they invest wisely and they do not succumb to all the trappings of an affluent lifestyle. They live by their means and make careful and wise decisions. They do buy, you just need to give great products and give them great client service as well as show your knowledge, kindness and expertise.

If ever you find yourself judging a potential client, think to yourself that you are stereotyping that person and indeed have no idea what they are all about or capable of buying?

Furthermore, you do not know who they know! I had a client I found an apartment for and while he didn't have the money to pay my commission, he has referred me business for new listings! Sometimes you have to do things because it is the right thing to do, not for the money. The bonus comes when it pays a handsome return in a way you never imaged.

If anyone is in need of your help, smile, be kind and make them feel welcomed by you ...always!

"The harder the conflict,

the more glorious

the triumph."

– Thomas Paine

Objection Handling

Every person's natural defense is to say no, in one way or the other. In fact, it is thought that the most successful people use the word "NO" more often than the average person. But still when you hear it, it stops you in your tracks. It brings you right back to when you were a child and your teacher or parent said no to you.

It feels awful and limiting...powerless and demeaning. All those things you yearn for in your adult life are cut short with this two-letter word. NO. I even sometimes get flush with defensive adrenaline when I hear it. Some people feel sick to their stomachs when they are told no. I am a yes person, so how can I live in a world where people tell me no?

Like everything in life, getting used to a no answer takes practice. The more familiar you are with dealing with a no answer, the more fun you can have with moving the no to a yes answer. It will become a game versus a car that came to a complete deal stop. You may not lose your breath so obviously. When you are ok with no, a smile comes across your face and that confidence you have tucked deep inside of you creeps up to the surface. Game on!

Often times they will not come out and say it as clear as NO, they will make excuses, delay the sale somehow by asking for even more information, etc. The truth of the matter is this is a big purchase and they may not have all the confidence they need in YOU to make this purchase.

Have you done your job properly? Do you speak with confidence offering them truthful insight to the properties? Make sure your confidence in YOURSELF and your ability to SELL is crystal clear. YOU CAN DO THIS! Heck you have a license to do this, this is your JOB and you have spent countless hours helping these people find a place to live. Enough is enough already it is time to get REAL. Any time you hear:

"I will think about it"

"Let me look online"

"Let's see what else is out there"

"I need to talk with my husband/ wife/ spouse / partner/ financial advisor/ mortgage broker"

"I don't like the countertops" – this one really gets me ...you are looking at a several hundred thousand property and you are picking out a $2,000 detail.   In this objection, you need to bring them back to reality with your granite statistics and have your installer reference from your tribe list ready to give them.   "Let's think about this...the property is worth $500k and you are concerned about the granite, MT AUBURN granite can install your countertops for $2,000....it is a minor detail in the big picture.

If they are still stuck on it, look creatively how to move past it. Well this house has a 2-car garage which was not on your Wishlist, but adds another $15k to the property value, you are already ahead of the game. Keep working and shaping the deal until you get your yes answer. Or if you feel this is not going anywhere, that they are lingering in the house for no apparent reason...cut bait and move on.

All of these are people's polite way of saying NO to you.

Now if you did your homework and offered them the information, I presented to you ...market statistics, options in their price range, meets all their criteria, they are already pre-approved for a loan...you can say to them with confidence:

"This property has all the features, the location, the price, everything you have asked for. I have given you more than enough information to make this decision right here and now".

If it's a yes, GREAT! Let's move on to the next.

If they are still wavering, cut bait and move on to the next property. And you may want to be sure at this point you have an exclusive listing document in place, because they can drop you and all your hard work as easily as they change their minds.

They keep changing their minds

If there is not a lot of inventory (apartments to rent or homes to sell) you can say with confidence, that if this meets at least 75% of what you are looking for, you need to put in an application today or make your offer. It is as simple as that. They do not have a lot of other options and most likely they can make the improvements they need to. They need a place to live and you found a great one for them. Now let's do this!

However, if they are in no hurry or have no major reason to move, they could just be wasting time. So be aware!

Know when to cut bait

Some people just like to waste time. I have no idea why but they do and they are out there and you are bound to come across at least one of them! They are not ready to buy or sell and perhaps they never will, so know how to quickly sum up your consumers. Maybe ask for a preapproval letter from their bank or mortgage lender. This will show you what they are qualified to buy...so you are not looking at $1million homes when they are only able to pay for and be approved by the bank for $400,000.

Or if it feels right, just go ahead and ask them to sign and exclusive agency agreement. Some agents only work as exclusive agents (you have a written contract saying that these buyers will only work with you, should they use another broker, you will earn your commission), while others believe that it isn't necessary. If someone wants to work with me, they will. However, I have spent a lot of time working with people who end up buying with another agent....this one is a call you need to make for yourself. What style best suits you?

What's she talking about, cut bait?

I live in a fishing town. To cut bait is a metaphor for leaving something you want behind; usually because it is too much work for what it will pay out, or simply deciding to let it go. It comes from the fishermen who have a catch on the line and have been working to reel the fish onto the boat. Sometimes, the line gets crossed or jammed or is not worth the effort, so they will cut the line losing the bait to the ocean.

You can always and should always cut bait if you feel a client is wasting your time. I don't mean give them up completely, but stop giving away your precious time and energy is this is not going anywhere. The timing is off, or whatever the deal. Keep them on a back file or add them to a monthly email campaign where you touch base every now and again, but focus on those clients who are ready to make a move and are actively listening to your input and working with you.

If you feel they are not realistic in their price range on the buy or sell side, give them a reality check by showing them comparative sales in their neighborhoods. Wake them up a bit and bring them back to reality. We all would love a brand-new Ferrari for the price of a VW Jetta, but it isn't happening.

If you simply do not have the time to dedicate to this type of client, refer them off to another agent and get a percentage split of the deal! Yes, that can actually happen! The rules may vary from office to office, but be sure to ask up front if they are open to splitting the deal and how much the lead would be worth to them. Then go ahead and make the introduction. Money in your bank account! You can get paid a percentage of the commission for referring over business, it happens between states (if you client is moving out of state and you are not licensed to sell in that state) and boundary lines for international deal and also within your own offices!

Wouldn't you want to work with someone that is referred to you?

If you find you are not able to communicate with them.

This happened when I was selling software. I had a client who I just could not communicate with. It sounded as if we were saying the same thing, but he could not understand me and I could not understand him. It was so bizarre because it was not hostile, we simply could not communicate with one another. I knew I wanted to help him and he was actively looking to purchase my software offering, our lines of communication were just completely jumbled.

In order to have my company keep the business, I asked another sales rep to kindly take over and see if she is able to make it happen. Sure enough they clicked, could clearly understand one another and the deal came shortly afterwards. Sometimes, even when speaking the same language, two people cannot understand each other and that is ok! Just be sure to recognize it and pass the client on sooner rather than later.

If the client isn't willing to follow your advice.

This is a tough situation. You want your client relationships to be cooperative and mutually beneficial. However, if you find yourself giving way more to the client and spinning your wheels ...as in they are not taking one single piece of advice you are giving them; cut bait and find another client who is a better fit for your style of sales.

If the client ever makes you feel unsafe or uncomfortable. You do not ever have to work with anyone you do not want to. I am not saying to run from anyone who poses a challenge to you or makes you feel uncomfortable from a knowledge or growth perspective, that is different. That is a learning curve and a confidence issue you need to take a look at and embrace within yourself. I am talking about clients who creep you out. The ones who you absolutely do not trust or feel safe around. Never put yourself at risk – EVER! Your health, wellness, happiness in life are the most important things here. Clients will come and go; therefore, if you ever feel those virtues are being compromised. CUT bait and leave!

"The more the merrier' he would say.

Your instincts in real estate, especially in dealing with people and negotiating will get sharper and sharper the more interactions you have. And these are all skills you leaned on the playground (plus a few thousand more) ...you got this. Trust your instincts but be open enough to want to grow and challenge yourself. You don't have to necessarily like all the people that you work with; however, you do need to find a common ground to do business with them. Keeping an open mind and heart in all of your transactions is essential to propelling your real estate business and career onward and upward.

Negotiating

Real estate is an active and live market. There are buyers, sellers, investors, interest rates, government and many other factors involved in each and every transaction. Negotiating is an art and the best negotiators are the ones who find WIN - WIN situations.

I personally do not like when people take advantage of one another, and it happens a lot in business and real estate. But what good is taking advantage of someone else? I feel there needs to be ethics involved as well. Make fair offers, and if your client is looking to take advantage, you can either decline to work with them. Or let the other agents know that they are going to submit a very low offer and that you hope to work word something that works for all parties.

Your job as an agent is to protect your client, to know your market statistics and to guide them in the process of buying or selling real estate.

The other piece of negotiating is learning to read people. Buyers and sellers both will tell you half-truths, or not explain everything. I worked with a landlord who all of a sudden would expect a contract on the spot when it had just been sent to me. He never specified a deadline; but had one in his mind. As an agent, you need to become adept at reading people and noticing peculiarities about people and human behavior. The more you interact with people, the more you will pick up on what they really mean.

Here is a scenario: your buyers have finally settled in on a house that they want to purchase. Rule number one is do not wait to put in the offer! As soon as possible be sure to have that offer written, signed and handed over the listing agent with a check / show of goodwill for the offer.

The offer will have a date on it of when that offer will expire, typically in 24 hours. You now have 24 hours to either have the offer accepted, or to negotiate a price that the sellers can be comfortable with selling their house for and your client able to afford. Make the offer as attractive as possible and be sure to attach a check for $500 or $1,000 as a show of good faith.

Closing the deal

Closing the deal is often times with seasoned REALTORs® say the work begins. There are a lot of moving parts at this point in the game, so you will want to work closely with your mentor or office manager to navigate this part of the process. This book is written to help with the marketing and ramping up of your business, but will give a very brief outline of the closing the deal process.

Write the offer: write up the offer for your client with a 24-hour deadline. This means the seller has 24 hours to review your offer, and either counter offer, accept or reject your offer. Keep in mind there may be several other offers being reviewed at the same time, so you want to be sure you write up a strong offer. Show that you have your financing in place with a pre-approval letter from your mortgage broker or proof of assets if paying by cash. Since real estate is such a personal business, sometimes buyers will attach a personal letter explaining how much they want to live here, a little bio about themselves and what their dreams for the property are.

Accepted offer: Once the offer is accepted, it is time to book the home inspection.

Inspection: Book the home inspection with someone you know and trust and be sure you are there when it happens. Some inspectors are more alarming than others, so it is good to be there to help your clients understand fully what information the inspector is relaying to them. It may be something very common that happens in old homes, but if they never heard of it, may sound like a big deal. Some of these inspections can last up to 5 hours or more, but you will learn so much about the house and your client will be thankful for your support.

Counter offer: On occasion, the home will not be exactly as it was described to the buyers. The windows may all need to be replaced, the inspector may have found termites or lead paint. This leads to a counteroffer in some cases. The buyer may write up a new offer or lesser value to reflect the costs it will take to bring the home to the level it was marketed as.

Financing: Get the financing in place. Work with your preferred mortgage broker, or your client may want to work directly with their bank. Have your client lock in their interest rate with their mortgage company.

Insurance: Insurance binder. Work with your insurance broker to be sure exactly what your buyers needs for their location. Take a look at these 3 widely held insurances:

Title insurance ensures both the lender and the owner's financial interests in the home are protected against loss due to title defects, liens, or other matters.

Homeowners insurance protects you from things like storms, fires, falling trees, structural damage to the home. If you own the home outright you can waive this insurance, but you are liable for all the replacement costs should damage occur.

Flood insurance protects the homeowner in case of flooding due to rising sea levels, rivers, or other types of water damage. in my seaside neighborhood, we all have to have flood insurance if the home is mortgaged. If the home is owned outright, you can waive it. But with the massive storms we have had of late, it may be worth carrying just in case.

Legal: The buyer's closing attorney will be there to sign over all the paperwork and to file it with the state. Ask around to friends, family and coworkers who they recommend to use for a closing attorney. From that list, give them a call and see who you best fit with. Read more about selecting a real estate closing attorneys in this article: https://www.wikihow.com/Select-a-Real-Estate-Attorney-for-a-Closing The closing attorney will work to have all the paperwork signed dated and recorded at the Registry of Deeds. Once it is recorded, your buyers are now homeowners!

Utilities: Advise your buyers and sellers to be sure to have the utilities signed over to the new owner. Any overages in fuel costs are usually split at the time of closing.

Congrats, your clients are now homeowners and you are officially a real estate agent with a successful closed sale!

"Do the one thing

you think

you cannot do.

Fail at it.

Try again.

Do better the second time.

The only people who never tumble

are those who never mount the high wire.

This is your moment.

Own it."

-Oprah Winfrey

Work Ethic

Staying in the game and keeping a positive attitude makes it all worth it. Trust me it pays off! This isn't a get rich quick profession. And if you find that it is, please write the book and I will buy & promote yours to learn and share your strategy.

For the rest of us, it takes time and dedication to succeed in this business. It is not a typical job where you go to work, are given or told what you need to get done, do some work and leave at the end of the week with a nice paycheck and benefits. No, you have to EARN every cent you take home and then pay for your own benefits and retirement.

The buck starts and stops all with you! Your time is precious, so be aware at what is taking you lots of time to do and not giving you results. Those are the areas you either need to outsource, practice to get better at or stop doing all together.

Do not fret, I am here to help you launch your successful careers with ideas to keep you busy and active for years.

Take one idea and implement it each week. Work with that skill. See how it feels, note the results you are getting and track your progress (if you like to keep score of your learning curve and results).

Continue to do that skill and introduce a new one the following week. You will build upon your positive work ethic and have a whole cadre of skills at your fingertips. It has been said that it takes 14 days to create a new habit, so stick with what you are trying and give it time to work!

It's hard to imagine in a digital age, but things do not always appear magically! They take time, effort and persistence. And in some cases, you need to give them some space to grow! But the first step is to begin with the new skill you want to try out.

As with anything new, it will feel awkward. You will find 100 other things to do than pick up that phone (if you are working on calling). You will make breakfast, the post office will need you, the dog will need to be walked.

Ignore all those responses and stay focused on your mission at hand. Go try out that new skill and see how it works for you!

By staying with the uncomfortable feeling, you will learn how to work with it, rather than avoid it. My brother Tom's family motto is "get comfortable with being uncomfortable" and he is right! In my holistic studies at SRU, we were trained to "lean into the resistance". Most people pull away from things that are uncomfortable and avoid the discomfort. When you lean into it, you accept it for what it is and take the control of the feeling or situation. You diffuse the situation and move into a position of control and acceptance.

It is a matter of moving beyond your fears - often times with calling, it is the fear of rejection, or getting your feelings hurt. Reframe the purpose of your calls - to offer information and a service to them and see if that helps!

Go ahead and focus, find that niche you want to work on and go for it!

"You are very powerful,

provided you know how powerful you are."

– Yogi Bhajan

Know Your Worth

Know Your Worth

Know your worth and be ready to tell your clients why they should use your professional skills as a REALTOR® versus anyone else's! You will most likely hear people ask why they should work with you? And you need to be ready to tell them what makes you so special! But in the meantime, here is a list of all the wonderful things we do for our clients (pretty much out of pocket) until their house is sold or found (if working with buyers). Very few professions in the world will let you work countless hours and not be guaranteed a cent ...because after all you only get paid if a house sells or closes.

The other thing is buyers and sellers often times think that it is easy to sell their own home; or that they do not need an agent. With the internet and easy access to listings everyone thinks that they are real estate agents. What they don't know is all the work that goes into selling and buying a home. Your job is to KNOW your worth and spread the word. This is what I will do for you and SPELL IT OUT FOR THEM.

My favorite is when a client will try to negotiate my fee right out of the gates. They will ask what is your rate? I tell them what I am willing to work for and they reply with a counter offer. "How about I give you a % less"? My answer is simple and it is always the same. If I am so eager to give up my commission, I sure as hell am not going to be fighting for your highest sale price (for sellers) or negotiating the best price for buyers.

It is that simple. Top sales people know their worth and they are not willing to compromise. Sorry. My time is valuable.

Keep in mind, most likely these very same people are not haggling with restaurants at dinner asking for a discount on their meals or with their doctors to get a discount on their checkups. Get real and know your worth.

Lastly before we get to the list is on average homes sell for 20% more when listed with a REALTOR®. REALTORS® know the ins and outs of the transactions and get the job done...putting more money in the seller's pockets

1) Real estate agents are your local real estate experts! We provide information from school and commuting, to yoga studios and restaurants. We are your "go to" person for recommendations!

2) We have insight to the market and what is coming on to perfectly match your home desires with listings that best suit your needs.

3) We run neighborhood comps and market "comps" or comparative market data to see what your home is worth in today's market.

4) Agents negotiate the terms of the sale and purchase, including any or all repairs, items that go along with the sale or any pricing concessions.

5) We are your educated voice.

6) We do not have an emotional attachment to the property which could hinder the sale.

7) We help you figure out your budget; how much of a mortgage you can receive / afford.

8) Agents can look over your credit report to be sure that you show your best when going for a mortgage.

9) Agents do all the leg work, especially with signing contracts!

10) We list your house in the MLS and bring it to market!

11) We host all of your open houses...or bring you around to them...scheduling, following up with sellers, or buyers.

12) We review all offers for sellers and write up offers for buyers!

13) Agents can draft your contract for you, or recommend a great real estate attorney to do so (go to your tribe)!

14) We arrange for all your inspections, including the pest and the carbon monoxide.

15) We help you find homeowners insurance (which is needed prior to closing the sale).

16) We order the title search on your property and hire surveyors to survey the property.

17) We are the sound barrier between multi party deals (husband and wife; buyer and seller; siblings).

18) We get the deal closed for you!

There are hundreds of other things you will end up doing for your clients - shutting off the water so their pipes don't burst for instance - so be sure to write them down! Make note of them, so next time you have a shred of doubt about your worth, you will stay strong and let that person know they are getting the better deal!

_____

_____

_____

_____

_____

_____

_____

_____

_____

_____

_____

_____

_____

_____

_____

_____

_____

_____

_____

_____

_____

_____

_____

_____

I AM WORTH IT!

100% PERCENT

"A journey of a thousand miles

must begin with

a single step."

-Lao Tzu

Homework time!

As real estate agents, we are licensed to sell in the state that licensed us; and in some instances, your state may hold reciprocity with other states, meaning you can sell in those states as well.

Check with your local Real Estate Board to see where this may apply. Links to all 50 states real estate boards are at the beginning of this book.

My point is, you have a wide pool to pull from. The houses on one street alone could keep you busy for years, so it is important that you focus your attention on a particular area or neighborhood when marketing your services.

Many will take whatever business comes your way, but in order to carve your special niche and really get your name out there, it makes sense to narrow the reach. And to know your limits! Quite honestly some clients are not worth your time. You will not be a good fit for them and they will make the process very difficult for you.

By narrowing in on your search, you are taking control of how you want your personal brand and your business to unfold. So where should you focus your attention?

Ask yourself these questions to help clarify your target market.

- What areas do I know best?

- What areas have new developments?

- Where are there great schools?

- What areas are close to public transportation?

- Where do you live?

- Where do your friends live?

- ▢ Where does your family live?

- ▢ Where is there new activity?

  - ▢ Are the homes in a neighborhood being done over?

  - ▢ Is a developer investing in a new shopping center or Whole Foods?

Know Your Market Statistics

How do I know my market when I just learned what a market is? You are probably more aware of your market than you know. Read up on what is happening both locally and nationally.

- ▢ Is there a new development being built nearby?

- ▢ What are the mortgage rates doing?

- ▢ Are the rates up or down?

- ▢ What is the government doing about it?

- ▢ Is it expensive to borrow money?

- ▢ How is our currency trading?

This is important to know if you are dealing with international clients.

Perhaps the Euro is trading stronger than the dollar, so a $1M USD home will be less to them in Euros ...and be a great place to invest their money should the markets turn.

What is the cost per thousand?? If you don't know this, go ask a mortgage broker. They live by this statistic. It basically breaks down what it will cost to buy a house in digestible bits. For instance, when negotiating a sale, you can break it down to dollars per day instead of looking at that huge chunk of money over 30 years.

For Interest only: Take the loan (1,000) and your interest rate 4.25% (.0425) and multiply them together (1,000 X .0425 = $42.50) Divide by the number of payments to be made (12 payments in a year) 42.50/12 = $3.54 a month. You can apply this formula to any loan amount and the rate of interest charged. So, if the house your client wants is $10,000 more than they intended on paying.... knowing the cost per thousand you can tell then that it will cost them an extra $35 per month for this house ...much easier to accept than the $10k figure.

It is a little trickier for amortized loans, as you will need to account for the term of the loan...so I think it is best just to ask your mortgage broker what it is and go with that. And make it a regular practice ...that way you get to know your mortgage broker better and can start building out your network of trusted professionals.

Is your local area in good shape? Is it safe? Are there developments or improvements happening.... what is going on in your neighborhood? Politics? How are the school systems? Are there many houses available for sale?

This is a service business so make sure you are offering your clients the best service possible...and that may mean by sharing the wealth with other professionals who can also help them!

"Not everything that can be counted counts,

and not everything that counts can be

counted".

-Albert Einstein

Sum Up A Property

What does it mean to sum a property? Simply put, it means what you think the house is worth (in your professional opinion). You must know your market data. $ per square feet is a good rule of thumb to know, especially in urban areas. Look that up in the MLS so you have a starting point.

People talk real estate all the time, what this house is going for, what that one sold for - and they are not even REALTORS®! You need to keep up with your local market and research what other towns homes are going for. Use that MLS to see sold deals versus what the listing prices were. Begin to create a database in your mid of how homes are priced in different areas.

You have gone to all of the recent broker open houses, so you know what other homes are selling for and have sold for. You know how long properties are staying on the market. You know the condition of the home. With all that in mind you should be able to put a value for a home together pretty quickly.

The quote above here from Albert Einstein reminds us of something very important. Sometimes there is more to it than what you see. Sometimes, the buyer sees something that you don't. Maybe you have been in a town too long and do not see how much it has improved and how valuable it is now. That being said, it is super important that you listen to your client carefully. There may be additional value that is intrinsic.

Perhaps the house you looked at comps, the condition of the house, acreage, everything and came up with a value of $300k for the house. However, you then learn that someone famous lived in this property at one point. That could spike the price up tremendously for a certain buyer. Begin to look beyond the obvious.

Know your comps

What is a comp? A Comp is a comparable property, something that is like the one you are listing or selling. They share similarities in size, acreage, style home and location. If the house you are listing is a 4 bedroom / 3 bathroom on 1.5 acres that was built in the 1960s, you want to search for other properties in the direct neighborhood that match it as best as you can.

What is going on locally? What has sold in your area recently that matches up with your listing.... acres, year built, bedrooms, baths, garage, renovations, etc... what did it sell for? How long was it on the market for? Did it sell for more or less than list price?

What is on the market now that matches your listing or desired type of home?

Log into the MLS and run a search:

- Pull the number of bedrooms
- Within a 10-mile radius (more or less depending on how densely populated the area is)
- Homes that sold, are contingent or pending
- Within the last 12 months

This search will pull up your most likely comparable properties. From there go through the photos to compare condition of the home, check the dates the homes were built, what they sold for.

Now you have good information to begin your conversation with your clients with.

Know your numbers

- $1 per thousand (ask your mortgage broker friend)
- Tax rate: find out how much the town charges you in taxes each quarter?
- Assessed
    - Always Always Always know the assessed value –this is value on the property the town uses to calculate your taxes.
- Acreage
    - How much land is there? Is it buildable? How is it zoned?
- Bedrooms/ bathrooms
    - How many of them are there? Are they legal? Closets?
- Basement/ Garage/ In- Law/ Barn / Shed
- Systems
    - Heating/ Sewerage or Septic/SMART home/ Alarms

Days on the market- houses that sit on the market for a long period of time are less likely to sell at asking price. After a week or two, a couple open houses everyone that is interested has seen the house and either likes it and made an offer, is not interested or is wondering now what is wrong with it?

Price to sell! They sellers will always want top dollar and it is YOUR JOB to tell them that you will position the home to fetch top dollar, but the market will dictate the selling price it always does.

If you overprice a home, no one will come to the open house except for the nosy neighbors and people will begin to wonder.

If you price the house right, you will need a police detail at the front because there will be so much traffic through the house. Buyers know their market...most of them have been looking at real estate for longer than you have been an agent. They often times know the market better than you do. So, when a home is priced right, it usually will not last the weekend. Offers will start to come rolling in!

Everyone wants a Ferrari on a Ford budget.... if only that were true!

We all watched the Big Short film (if you haven't I would highly recommend it) and saw what happened a few years ago when the mortgage markets inflated real estate values.... let's get real folks!

If you have not watched 'The Big Short' you should. It will give you a quick education on the mortgage markets.

"Whatever course you decide upon,

there is always someone

to tell you that you are wrong.

There are always difficulties arising

which tempt you to believe that your critics
are right.

To map out a course of action

and follow it to an end

requires courage."

– Ralph Waldo Emerson

Ask for the business

One of the single most important things in closing a sale is asking for the business. This alone is what separates the successful salespeople and those who just let time pass them by. If you have someone interested in the home or need help searching for a home ...ask them for their business.

"I would love to earn your business; may I have your contact information and we can set aside some time to discuss your ideal home. From there I can pull together what I think match that description and you can tell me which ones you would like to tour". Does that work for you Mr. or Miss prospect? Yes, well great how does tomorrow at 11am sound? My office is perfect if that works for you?

Look at Frederick Eklund...the zany guy from Bravo's hit series Million Dollar Listing NYC. He is relentless in his pursuit of finding, closing, and getting more business. He is always looking for the next deal and how to maximize his current opportunities. Why sell one condo when you can ask the builder to represent the entire development....skyrocketing your name, brand, and earnings by asking for the business. If he is offered to sell 2 units in a condo development, he will meet with the financiers and the builders to get the whole entire building under his control. He doesn't just want a piece of the pie; he wants the whole pie! Now this may not be your style, but it is an example of someone who puts it all on the line to build his real estate business and consistently earn new business.

Additionally, you may have been working with a client for several months and all of a sudden, they go dark on you? What happened? Give yourself permission to ask for their business? Is everything ok? Are you still interested in putting in an offer on Elm Street? Do not let a deal run away from you. There is a fine balance between bothering someone and getting an answer, so be respectful, but know that you also deserve an answer.

Chapter Eight

Working with Sellers

WORKING WITH SELLERS

Congrats: you got the listing!

Now What?   Get it in writing!

You get the call or you bump into someone and they tell you that they want you to sell their house. Now what do you do? Get it in writing as quickly as possible. The first step is to have the sellers sign an exclusive listing agent agreement. This will lock you in as their real estate agent and prevent any other agents from getting this listing. Some REALTORS® I know roll the dice with this and do not require the form to be signed off on, but I think it is better to be safe than sorry. Get it signed.

Next, set up a time to preview the property. Do a quick walk through to be acquainted with the house. Make a list of what you see: type of roofing, siding, are the windows new or old, the condition of the kitchen and the yard, wall colors, things that stand out like cracks in the walls or uneven floors.

Ask them to put together a list of any improvements they did to the house since they owned it and dates of when they were done. This will help when putting the valuation together. Make note of the types of floors, condition of the appliances, is their carpet or hardwood floors, is the roof in disrepair, is the deck in good shape, do the faucets run properly, does the house look like it is in good working condition? Find out what they have recently invested in the home to keep it in great shape. Have they replaced the heating system or added solar panels? Ask these questions to get the best information about the house.

Listing Proposal

You will want to put together some sort of presentation, either online or a hard copy of one highlighting the benefits of working with you and your brokerage firm. If you are with a national brokerage like a Century 21, Coldwell Banker or REMax the brokerage you partner with should already have a slide deck together for you to do a listing presentation for your client. If they do not, you can easily create one. You will want to give information about:

☐ Brokerage (how long in business, # clients, revenue, etc).

☐ You (who you are, success you have had, what is the advantage of choosing you?)

☐ What you will do for your client - marketing, websites, emails, postcard.

☐ How your partners are for mortgages, insurance, inspections, etc

☐ Market data - info about the neighborhood & town the property is located in.

☐ Comps - other similar properties on the market (for sale now), a couple that have sold and some that are continent (in the process of being sold/ have an accepted offer.

☐ What they need to do to prepare the house for sale.

☐ A Timeline of events.

☐ Next Steps.

This is a lot of information to go through and most of them just want to know what you think they can get for their house. But find out what works best for you when presenting this information and go from there. **ON EACH SLIDE, SHOW THEM WHY THIS IS IMPORTANT TO THEM AND GET THEIR FEEDBACK AND AGREEMENT ON EACH ITEM.** You are building your value here and getting them to validate that what you are presenting is important to them. Let them bring up their objections now so you can clear them.

Make it crystal clear. You do not want to blow through this presentation thinking your potential clients understand what you are saying when it is highly likely they do not. Take the time to be sure they are on board and following along. The work you will be doing for them is important enough for their attention and will help with their understanding of your value when it comes time to talk about the commission. This is the start of the sales process so show your professionalism and command their attention.

Closing the deal for the listing

When delivering a closing question; "with all that I have shown you about the strength of my company, are you ready to sin the paperwork to list your house with me right now"? STAY SILENT AFTER DELIVERING this closing question. The client has all the information they need to make a decision at this point and your silence gives them the space to process, feel the uncomfortableness of the silence (if there are any) and make a YES decision. DO NOT break this silence. You have already asked your questions, now it is your turn to remain absolutely silent until the client speaks their YES answer.

Listing Paperwork

Paperwork, paperwork, paperwork...there is a lot of paperwork necessary to secure a listing ...and make sure it is all signed and dated properly.

My manager, Donna is excellent at hosting paperwork trainings for new hires. She gave us each copies of all the major forms and we went through them all filling out a master sample for us to keep in our binders for future reference. Mark it up, or you need to...x or sticker or arrow where you need signatures or set it up in your Docusign software...and make sure your admin or manager reviews it before so that you look like you know what you are doing and are relaxed!

There are several documents you will need to present to the seller in order to secure the listing. This will vary from state to state and by office, so check with your broker beforehand on all the paperwork that needs to be completed and how they want it submitted.

Most offices use eDocs or an online software that allows you to prepopulate (or fill in the unique details about the home) in advance and email it over to your clients for digital signatures. Right now, this seems to be the most secure way to capture this information, and store it safely.

"The question I ask myself

like almost every day is,

'Am I doing

the most important thing

I could be doing?'"

- Mark Zuckerberg

Prospecting for listings

By now you may have had some wins and losses, but with owning your own business once a deal closes, you are back at square one! Asking yourself, how do I get into this real estate game? Listings by far are the way to go! When you have the listing, your name is on the front lawn of a home for several days (sometimes months), which is free advertising. And, you also have the ability to capture the commission by finding the buyer as well. Full commission is the way to go!

So how do I get a listing? The list below highlights some ways to get a real estate listing. They are not in any particular order. Some methods will work better for you and your personality than others, so give them each a try and see what works.

- Cold calling

- Networking

- Emailing

- Meet & Greets

- Work another agent's open houses

- Facebook and Internet

- Direct Mailing

- Social Media

- Referrals

- BNI Meetings

15 Steps of a Listing

Technically this should be a 3-step process: get the listing, market the listing, and close the listing (close the sale). But you will see there are several pieces of the puzzle that need to be covered in between those steps.

1) PROSPECT FOR APPOINTMENTS (LISTINGS)

What the heck is prospecting? Like back in the early 1900s when everyone headed to California to pan for gold...that is what prospecting is about in more ways than one. Prospecting is about uncovering leads and potential clients through a multitude of activities including: phone calls, emails, social media, networking event, mailing letters, advertisements, etc. Anything you do in order to secure a client would fall under prospecting. You are digging for gold - literally.

2) SET QUALITY APPOINTMENTS

Once you discover that your lead is interested in your help, make an appointment to meet with them and discuss their needs including their budget, what they are preapproved for, location, home style, etc... with your sellers meet with them to discuss their timeframe to sell, an idea of what they want to receive for the home, etc.

3) PROPERTY REVIEW

Always be sure to PREVIEW THE HOME. You do not know what you are dealing with until you see it for yourself. Do not talk market stats, or commission, nothing, just see the house and get the details and confirm the facts. A quick view to see what condition the house is in and to show you are ready to get it sold.

4)   SET APPOINTMENT #2

Call, email text however you choose to communicate with your potential client, and set a date and time on the calendar to meet with them in person to speak one on one about real estate. In this meeting, you will dive deeper into the history of their property, so ask them to make a list of all the upgrades they have done since they purchased the house.

5)   RESEARCH AND PREPARE

You are just starting out, so you will not know everything and that is ok. However, you do want to know enough to be dangerous. Do your best to do some research online, ask your mentor or manager and know your info before going to the meeting. What did the house sell for before, what are the taxes, when was it built, what is the zoning? What is the neighborhood like? What amenities does the neighborhood have? Is there an annual festival? Do tourists come to this area to visit? What makes this place such a great place to live? Maybe it is an easy commute to the city. Have your list of important question you want answered prior to taking the listing.

6)   PRE-LISTING MARKETING MATERIALS

Your goal is to win this listing opportunity. Some people are brilliant at talking their way through things, and closing business on the fly. Most others need some backup. Bring some marketing collateral from your office. Have your marketing information available in an online presentation or in printed handouts or booklets including details about your brokerage firm and why they are successful, outline what services you will offer your client, personal introduction page, and cards. As you win more and more listings, keep a record of each house that you listed and sold, including how long it took to sell and what price it sent for versus the listing price. For my sports fans, it is like keeping track of a batting average.

7)   LISTING PRESENTATION

This is what you will use to win the business! In your slide deck show what makes you the best person to present them, the market comps, what you can do for them, etc. What is your goal for the meeting? List of further questions? Just thinking for later? What would you like to see as the best possible outcome? In addition to that, is there anything else you are looking for?   If we are able to meet those goals are you prepared to begin marketing your property today?

- ☐   Dedicated to your real estate needs

- ☐   To sell your property quickly & for the most money!

- ☐   Strategic, creative & resourceful

- ☐   Fast response rate

- ☐   Strong negotiator

- ☐   Wide network of over 5,000+ followers

- ☐   Social media maven

- ☐   Education

- ☐   Awards and credentials

- ☐   Email

☐   Cell number

☐   Personal Website

This is a marketing business. Sell yourself first! Make yourself stand out from all other agents out there. Then, walk them through all the programs that you offer that can benefit them with your marketing materials. Make sure they are crystal clear on what you are offering to do for them... do not move past MARKETING. Get their agreement to the marketing right away! One of my sales training taught me to get the buyer in the habit of saying yes. The more they are saying yes to each of the slides you are presenting, the more likely they are to say yes to you as their listing agent!

Once they have agreed to your marketing plan, that is then the price conversation starts. Before you blurt out a number, position your reasoning of how and why you came up with the number you did. Highlight the importance of pricing the house correctly, types of markets (buyers and sellers), pricing within individual marketplaces, what's happening with their specific house based upon its condition.

Price: What I charge has nothing to do with the price of your house. The price is what the price is. Let us get that settled.

Fee: takes place in the listing paperwork. Get them to agree to work with me first. Fill out the listing contract first and STATE IT AS A FACT. Name address, permission, the listing commission is YOUR PERCENT (ask for what you are worth) you will owe us for all my service,

So, they have decided to move ahead with you are their agent. You have won their confidence and their listing. Now it is time to get this place in tip top selling shape! Most sellers do not want to invest much money in a home they are leaving, however sometimes small investments like painting walls and mowing lawns can reap large returns. It is time to depersonalize the home and make it into a place where someone else would love to live!

9)   STAGING

Declutter the house, paint the front door, make space for FLOW in the house, or full-blown staging. The goal is to neutralize the home to the point where it looks showroom but livable. Read through the staging section for more tips on staging to sell! See the section on "setting the space" for more details.

10)   COMMUNICATE

Stay in touch with your clients throughout this process. Just because you are doing a ton of work, does not mean that they know you are doing all of this good work for them. So, let them know! Make it a point to check in daily, or at least bi weekly to share what offers came in, what feedback you are getting on the home, what you have done for signage and marketing.

11)   RESPOSITION

If the house has been on the market for a few weeks and is not gaining interest from prospective buyers, you will want to meet with your client and discuss repositioning the property. This could mean a price adjustment, a marketing adjustment, or a new approach. Take notes on what feedback you are getting from other REALTORS® and from prospective buyers. Perhaps the chimney needs to be repointed and you didn't pick up on that - it could cost thousands of dollars for the new homeowner to get it to working condition. Make a note and let the sellers know. They say, if the house does not sell in the first two weeks, then most likely it was priced wrong.

12)   NEGOTIATE

Someone wants to buy the house! The offer is in... now it is time to negotiate. Send all offers to your clients, and give them your insight on the offers to help them read all offers clearly. One may be a lower number but all cash - that signals a potentially easier close. One may be a higher price offer, but they want to add a contingency of sale of another property ...that is a weaker offer. Weigh out each offer separately and have your clients do the same. Remind them to not take this personally if the offers are low. Talk with the buyer's agent to see why they think the house is worth so little?   If you refuse one offer, be sure to let them know that should anything not work out with the chosen buyer, you will call them immediately. Deals fall apart so be sure to keep all interested parties in the loop.

13)   MANAGE YOUR TRANSACTION

There are several documents and papers that are signed during this process, so your job is to make it as smooth as possible for your client. Optimal client experience is what we are aiming for here! If possible, use your Zipforms or other online forms to facilitate the process. The software makes it so easy to show where the parties need to sign and date.

14)   CLOSE THE DEAL

Come in and sign and close it up with the closing attorneys. Also called 'passing the papers'. The attorneys typically lead all for this. You will come up with a date and time that all parties are able to meet and the lawyer will run through all the documents that needs to be signed, collect all payments necessary and divvy up any monies to be split at the close of the deal. This may include fuel fees for paid overages remitted to the seller. In MA it is not required that the buyer's agent attend this meeting, but I feel it is a good thing to be there to be sure everything goes smoothly. Once everything is signed, the attorney will file the documents with the Registry of Deeds. This is when the deal is final.

15)   FOLLOW UP WITH YOUR CLIENTS

This is a people business. Create a GREAT follow up system and put it in place...use your broker database to log and schedule calls or any sort of calendar app or scheduling app you need to stay on track. Keep them close so that they will be your client again and again...talk to them, reach out to them. Consider sending them a small thank you gift, send emails with market news, etc. Also, it helps to have positive reviews to put on your website or facebook page, so talk to your clients and see how they felt you did as their agent. Ask them if they would be willing to write a review for you and post it!

RESEARCH AND PREPARATION

Go to Town Hall

Why should I go all the way to Town Hall, when I can look it up online? True, yes that may indeed be true, but trust me you want to get to know these people. Talk to the tax assessors, building inspectors, department of health to check on the septic system (they record and can you tell every time the septic is pumped) less than twice a year is considered failed. Introduce yourself, ask them questions, and get to know who does what for the towns you operate in.

When you have a question from your client, or need something done, you will know who to go to and they will know and recognize you. Who knows they may even be more likely to refer you! Some agents will bring coffee or snacks into Town Hall as a thank you for their help. Most agents do not set foot in the town hall.

The city clerk is who you go to in order to find out have the taxes been paid? Make sure the lot has been recorded.

Go through the plat books. Learn the actual boundaries and acreage.

Additionally, you will get to know the people there, they see me and know I am active in the area....my tribe!

- Board of Assessors

- Board of Health

- Building Department

- Conservation Commission

- Historical Commission

- Planning Department and board

When selling, it isn't all about presenting. For instance, the open house.

Find out what they are looking for before they start their tour and when signing in. That way as you take them around you can validate that what this house has to offer is exactly what they are looking for. SHOW THE BENEFIT OF EACH THING WE DO AND GET APPROVAL ON EACH THING WE DO BEFORE I MOVE ON TO THE NEXT ITEM

In sales, we call this:

Feature – Benefit – Approval

The first 30 days are the MOST IMPORTANT time of a listing, make sure that the property is PRICED correctly.

- Ask deeper level questions. When you present something, like the CONSULT through questioning

- Educate: enlighten them on your process and what services you will provide.

- Marketing: what is going on in the region, their town, statistic, then talk about their house in particular.

- Price: check other comparable properties and agree to a price.

- Commission: earn your worth.

GET PAPERWORK SIGNED

Go through all your listing documents. These vary by state, so check with you mentor or your office to see what forms are required by your state.

SIGNAGE

MAKE SURE THE SIGN HAS BEEN POSTED ON THE LAWN with your broker's name, your name, your photo and your phone number. This is the best advertisement you will ever get. Someone allowing your name, face and contact information be outside of their home on their front lawn for an extended period of time. It does not get any better than this!

Add the listing to the MLS so all agents are aware this property is coming to market. We want to get as many people as we can excited about the listing - so marketing is the key!

Writing Up the Listing in MLS

Words and photos are what will catch people's attention and bring your buyers in. So be creative but accurate with your wording of the listings. Notice the language their agents use. You can almost feel like you are there without evening seeing a photo of the place.   Become familiar with what is necessary and what isn't.   Like my high school English teacher Mrs. Middleton used to say – "if it doesn't hold value and add to the story, take it out". Choose your words carefully and if needed, ask for help from a ghost writer. Here are some luxury listings for you to take a look at:

Spectacular parlor triplex by one of South End's premier developers, Renaissance Investments. Open concept living/dining/kitchen highlighted by 10'7" high ceilings, custom moldings, fireplace and woodwork on the main level. Featuring state-of-the-art chef's kitchen including Wolf Range and vented ceiling hood, Sub-zero refrigerator/freezer, Marvel beverage center, custom cabinetry, waterfall island, and hardwood floors. Dining room showcases a herringbone hardwood floor for added elegance. Master bedroom with Juliette balcony, walk-in closet, master bath with dual shower heads and rain shower, leathered marble dual vanity and radiant flooring. Two sun-filled guest bedrooms have ensuite baths with quartz vanity, shower surrounds in onyx tiling, tile floors. generous closet space, hardwood floors and views. Family room with wet bar and fireplace leads out to magnificent landscaped private patio. Garage parking is available for either sale or rental; ask agent for details.

The ultimate trophy compound and a true work of art in the coveted "Bird Streets" above the Sunset Strip. Located on a quiet cul-de-sac, this stunning property offers sweeping views from downtown to the ocean. American walnut flooring throughout 5 bedrooms, 6 baths, a theater and gym. Spacious master w/ skylights, large closets & separate handbag & shoe rooms. Top-of-the-line Italian kitchen w/ Thermador appliances, Caesarstone counter-tops, 2 ovens & 2 dishwashers. Dining area includes Tiffany dining table & Delfin swivel chairs. Home theater with seating for 10 features plush reclining sofas, LED lighting and home automation. The outdoor space hosts an 1800 sq.ft. infinity pool, 8ft. fire pit & alfresco dining areas and more.

This historic Gold Coast graystone offers grand living space ideally suited for entertaining and city living. It's on one of the neighborhood's prettiest blocks, close to the park, lakefront, Michigan Avenue and downtown. A labor of love, this 8,600 sqft, four-level residence was renovated from top-to-bottom, resulting in a tasteful blend of superior quality craftsmanship and modern convenience. The herringbone hardwood floors, oversized crown molding and custom staircase are exceptional. A handsome living, dining and family rooms are ideal for entertaining. The top-quality eat-in kitchen opens to an English conservatory and blue stone terrace. The second level was designed as a luxurious full floor master suite, with two additional bedrooms and a library on the 3rd level. The lower level includes a 4th bedroom suite, home theater, exercise room, catering kitchen and ample storage. Other features include an attached 2-car garage and landscaped gardens with an in-ground watering system.

Coffee on the patio or cocktails on the upper balcony overlooking the 14th green of Tour 18, wow! Incredible features from the front circle drive to the exercise center complete with sauna off the master suite with separate entry. Enjoy the Sport Court for basketball or tennis, or use the foundation to build an extra garage, office or mother-in-law suite. Cozy up to four different fireplaces (one outdoor), hand carved mantels, and generous crown moldings. On to the chef's kitchen and abundance of counter space to a wine room cellar to hold a lifetime of bubbly. Want to design a backyard water feature? Seller offering $25k to get it started for full price offer! Close to private Liberty Christian School.

Don't miss this impeccably designed custom-built home, and the oasis you'll find out back. Traditional design elements paired with transitional decor create an elegant, relaxing home. Outside awaits a heated, saltwater pool & spa, professionally designed & maintained landscape, irrigation & lighting. 3 bedrooms with large walk-in closets & bonus room upstairs. Downstairs master suite & adjacent study or 5th bedroom/nursery. Walk-in attic + Pull-down attic + Carport Storage. Ask for full list of features!

Private colonial on 3.6 Acres! Farmers porch leads you in to large living and great rooms which bookend the open concept living space. 3 Bedrooms and 2.5 baths and Brand New 4 Bedroom septic so ready to expand as needed! Also New heating system, water heater, washer/dryer

Escape to the beach! This light-filled beach house is just what you need to let go and relax. Only steps away from the ocean and walking distance to local island eateries. Our beach cottage has been renovated and updated, including a stunning outdoor shower. The downstairs has one

Newly Renovated: You enter into the open concept living space with spacious living & dining area. The kitchen has brand new white cabinetry, new Samsung appliances, quartz counter tops and a PANTRY. There is a half bathroom on the first level with laundry hookups.

Your dreams are about to come true! How you ask? This fabulous custom built open concept French country farmhouse with wrap around porch on a lush landscaped corner lot in Amesbury's most sought after neighborhood, Merrimack Landing is ready for you to call home! A true chefs kitchen...

Love where you live! Gilbert St has been declared a Scenic Road - we'd like to invite you over to see why! Sweets Pond, Otis St. Baseball & Soccer fields, & even the famous Old County Store where you can still buy Penny candy & listen to the coin operated player piano is just a short......

PERFECT FOR BUYERS SEEKING DISTINCTIVE HOME WITHOUT MA STICKER PRICE! Custom & Private. A 750 ft drive, professionally landscaped w/ 60+ planting varieties and 1800 foot stone wall. Peaceful surroundings on mahogany farmers porch or oversized southern facing deck.

A rare, historic offering. Built in 1790, this remarkable 4 Bed/3 Bath Colonial sits proudly on .59 acres of luscious trees, garden areas, flowers and tranquility. Set back and quiet, in-ground heated pool, pool shed, koi pond, 2 car garage, and a gym flank the perimeters of the

Getting ready for the open house

Ideally, the goal is to never have to even have an open house. You should use your network so well that it sells prior to the open. So, work on those networking skills!

If you do have an open house, your goal is to have ready buyers come through! In order to build up anticipation of the event, you can:

- Post the open house date and time notice on the yard sign.
- Host a broker open house the week before the public open house.
- Create an "event" for the open house on your facebook page for your friends and clients to see. And you can share the event with larger town groups who may be interested on facebook.

Make sure when you agree to take a listing, you have your sellers commit to doing their side of the business and a big part of that is cleaning out their house and staging it to sell.

Can cluttered homes be sold? Absolutely! But you will not fetch top dollar bids you would if you spent a couple days cleaning up, painting, or even refinishing floors if you have a pet that has destroyed them. A client sold their home in one day well over asking price (when there were many similar homes on the market for sale) and it is because of how beautiful and "move in ready" the house looked.

Photo by Mark McCammon from Pexels

"Have nothing in your houses

that you do not know to be useful,

or believe to be beautiful."

-William Morris

Clear out all the clutter

For some people clearing away clutter can be an emotional process, but once it is done, it feels so great to have more space in your home. A client recently told me after he cleared his house to rent it, he wanted to move in! Hire a dumpster if you need to and be realistic about the time it can take to clear out the house.

How long clearing clutter will take all depends on several factors including, how much stuff you have to get rid of, how you want to get rid of it, how good you are at tossing things you no longer need. If you feel emotionally attached to your items, it may be helpful to have a friend help you out. If you are not using something, then it is not "of use" to you, so get rid of it and make some space in your life some something better!

I highly recommend any home owner or person ready to downsize to read "The Life Changing Magic of Tidying Up: the Japanese art of decluttering and organizing".

The author, Marie Kondo shares with us her expertise in helping thousands of people to remove items that "no longer spark joy" and find a "dramatic reorganization of the home (which) causes correspondingly dramatic changes in lifestyle and perspective. It is life transforming. "

Not all of us live in a home ready to be photographed for the pages of Elle Décor, but we can take steps to move towards a picture-perfect existence.

Marie further suggests you, "start by discarding". To do so, you need to sort and purge with:":

☐   Dumpster and getting rid of all unwanted items

☐   Having yard sales

☐   Calling your antiques dealer to appraise and sell your valuables at auction

☐   Bring items to a consignment shop for clothes, furniture or antiques

☐   A shredder to shred all old documents

For the do it yourself person:

☐   Use eBay to sell unused items www.eBay.com

☐   Facebook yard sale sites for your town

☐   Mercari and PoshMark for your clothing and beauty products

☐   Craigslist www.craigslist.org

☐   A poster or email in your post office with items for sale

☐   Hire a company like EBTH "everything but the house" to consign your items www.ebth.com

Anything that does not sell, donate it. There is the Goodwill Industries, American Veterans, Big Brother and Big Sister, these are to make a few nonprofit organizations that resell the items that you no longer use to raise money for their causes. Most of these organizations will even come to your house for a scheduled pickup of goods. In addition, you receive a receipt to claim the donations as a deduction on your tax return (assuming you itemize your deductions).

Marie suggests that once most items have been discarded (and by discarded she means the ones that are no longer being used, or ones that no longer spark joy in your life); to then "organize your space, thoroughly, completely, in one go." This may not be your skill set. I know my artist and creative friends often times feel more comfortable in a less than perfect living space – some may call that messy, but it is their comfort zone. In those cases, you may want to have your buyers consult with a professional organizer. Someone who can go into the home create a document of all the recommendation of what they think will make the home show its best and them provide you with that document.

Some organizers charge between $100-300 for this service and additional costs based upon what work you want them to do from the report. A sample report would look include some of the following:

- Paint the outside fence

- Replace the mailbox

- Paint or replace the numbers on the house

- Paint the front door

- Replace front door handle

- Do some outdoor plantings or mulch

- Other landscaping suggestions

- Replace the broken windows

- Refinish hardwood floors

- ☐ Paint interior walls a neutral color

- ☐ Replace refrigerator

- ☐ Finish off the basement

Based upon the suggestions given, the owner can decide whether to do the work themselves, have other contractors (your tribe of recommended professionals) do the work, the organizer, or just choose not to do the work. The amount of work they want to put into selling their home will vary from person to person and home to home, however it is important as a professional to show them what they need to do in order to get their home ready to sell for top dollar. If they are willing to settle for less than that, well then just do your best to tidy up and sell around the clutter.

What does sell around the clutter mean? It means looking beyond the condition of the house and sharing with potential buyers' ideas you have of what can be done with the house. This works with people who are handy or know someone who can help with the work they will be doing. This also usually means that your listing will not sell for what other comps have sold upon that have done all the work and are move in ready.

To end this section on a mindfulness, note, Marie Kondo notes that people who use this method to remove clutter and organize their life will

"Begin to see a pattern in (their) ownership of things, a pattern that falls into one of three categories: attachment to the past, desire for stability in the future, or a combination of both. It's important to understand your ownership pattern because it is an expression of the values that guide your life. The question of what you want to own

is actually the question of how you want to live your life." - M. Kondo

Be aware of what you really need, and why you buy things for other reasons like boredom, habit or as therapy for your unmet emotions. Be aware of why you shop and keep a mental note of those triggers. Start to become comfortable with having less. Less items do not mean a lesser quality of life, rather a richer and more purposeful one.

Collect moments, not things.

Depersonalize the home

This can be one of the most challenging things a seller has to do. Think about it, they spent years making this home exactly how they want it. Now, you come in and tell them they have to take down their photo family history from the living room wall.

Buyers want to imagine what it will be like to live in this home. Seeing too much of the current owners is a distraction and a turn off. Be sure to take personal photos down, remove personal paintings or artwork, even personal papers.

Make the house less the current owners and more what it could be!

"All homes need staging.

There is no price range

where it doesn't work

and no price range that

doesn't want more money."

- Barb Schwartz

Stage the house to sell

Why should we bother staging the house?

Simple answer is to sell it fast!   If a home is unoccupied it is pretty easy to do ...homes are unoccupied mostly if it is a home that passed through an estate (someone inherited a property from someone who passed); if it is a second home, if it is in foreclosure, there are many reasons why a home could be vacant. However, it is easy to stage and maintain the staging of a vacant home.

When the home is bare, it is a blank canvas for your staging company, designer friend, family member, design student or whoever you trust with this vision to create. You or the homeowner will sign a contract with the terms and fees of the items being used to stage the home. This can run $500-$5,000+ per month depending on the scale of the project.

If the home is lived in: make sure the sellers have the home available within an hour's notice to show. That means:

- All beds made

- Wash & put always all dishes in the sink

- Floors swept & Rugs Vacuumed

- Counters cleaned

- Pets cleared from the home (no cats jumping out)

- All odors removed from the living space

- Papers cleared

- Clothing and toys picked up and put in a closet or in bins (buyers look in closets)

The 5 Golden rules of staging a home:

1. De-personalize: Less of you, more of them!

2. Maximize: Declutter to maximize the space

3. Sanitize: Clean it up people!   This is your ultimate first date.

4. Modernize: See what updates can be done on a dime.

5. Neutralize: Be Switzerland!   Neutral color palette, neutral style.

Setting the Space

To paint or not to paint? What updates need to be made? Is the house move in ready or a hoarder's dream? Whatever the condition it is YOUR JOB to show the house at its best!

Do you need landscaping? Maybe it just snowed and that covers a not so pretty yard....

Small improvements = big results!

Often times, I am asked what are some little things I can do to increase my home's value. We all know that BIG things ...update the kitchen and appliances, landscape, replace floors, add granite or quartz counters...sure with a huge budget, I can do that. But what are some things that will not break the bank that we can easily do?

Some quick and easy ways to make your home more appealing include:

- ☐ Paint your mailbox.

- ☐ Paint the interior walls a neutral color.

- ☐ Open the shades and let the light in!

- ☐ Clear out the clutter

- ☐ Freshen the air with a candle or indoor fragrance.

- ☐ Clean up the yard (shovel, rake, plant some grass or flowers).

☐ Freshen up with some new pillows for the couch.

☐ Clean up all pet and other odors.

☐ Fold and put away all laundry.

☐ Fluff up all decorative pillows and cushions.

☐ Place some fresh flowers in a vase.

☐ Paint the cellar and garage floors.

☐ Use some aromatherapy air diffusers: try rosemary or citrus to awaken!

☐ Be happy to show and sell your home!

What can a little paint do for me?

The Zillow Paint Colors Analysis measured how different paint colors in various room types may affect the sale price of a home compared to its Zestimate. They analyzed "more than 135,000 photos from listings around that country that sold between January 2010 and May 2018 to identify which paint colors were associated with a home selling for more or less than its Zestimate when compared to similar homes with white walls. The analysis controlled for other wall colors within each room type, square footage, home age, and ZIP code Zillow Home Value Index in the listing month. Price effects for different room-color combinations are estimates of the average premium or discount but may not reflect a causal difference in value compared to white walls".

Front door = black will boost sales by 2.9%

Living Room = pinkish taupe will help your sale pop!

Bathroom = periwinkle blue

Kitchen = black & white tuxedo (black cabinets/ counters) light walls & floors

For more information visit: https://www.zillow.com/research/paint-colors-help-sell-20240/

Great Photos

Let's face it, we live in a visual world; and the old adage, a picture speaks a thousand words is so very true in real estate. The photos you take (if you are shooting the home yourself) or that your photographer takes, should be clear and focused, taken under natural light if possible and accurately depict the house you are representing.

Sellers absolutely hate it when they see pictures of a house online, get all excited about it and start to imagine themselves and their family living there. They pack everyone up on their only free Saturday or Sunday of the year and walk into a house that looks nothing like what they saw online. It is misleading and it is unfair to your sellers to oversell their home.

I had this happen to me when I was working with buyers. I was showing them a historic home (the home was over 200 years old) and the listing stated that. However, the photos the listing agent listed made the house look like it had been totally renovated. Not sure what filter they used, but it did not match. The buyers were really upset that the house was "not new" like the "photos said". Because of the other agent's photos, I lost credibility with my buyers and lost their business.

It is one thing to include builder sketches or landscape design plans, but make clear note that these are suggestions and not how the property currently looks.

Bottom line is clear well taken photos with great natural lighting will show your listing best.

Lockbox or no lockbox?

I suggest always having a lockbox on the house. Trust me I tried it once without a lockbox and it was not fun for me or the owners. Each time I needed access to the house, I had to call or text the owner, and wait for their response. Sometimes it took an extra day or two to hear back from the owner whether or not I could show it and when. This is never good in a hot buyers' market.

Time is of the essence so get those showings done at once, or else your buyers will move on to their next choice! Now they were living in their home so some lead time is needed, but when the house was vacant when the owners were at work, I could have easily shown the home.

Lockboxes make showings that much easier to do! Once installed make sure you know how to use the lockbox. Be sure to give the lock box you select to use a test run. Much like your locker in high school, these can be cumbersome and difficult to figure out.

They can be tricky and in dark winter months at freezing temperatures, you must be sure you have tested this thing inside rather than with a frozen lockbox outdoors. Check with your brokerage to see if they have a lockbox you can use or you can purchase one of your own (or more than one if you are rally rocking your rookie year and have numerous listings going) at Home Depot for about $28 www.homedepot.com or at http://www.mfssupply.com/Contractors/Numeric-Lock-Boxes-Contractor for $12 or less depending on how many you purchase.

If there is an ALARM system, make sure you know how to use it, or how to deactivate it. The last thing you want on your pre-open house to do list is have the whole neighborhood and police on site...

"You never get a second chance

to make a first impression."

-Oscar Wilde

Conducting the open house

Arrive early (30-45 minutes I think is good) to walk around the outside of the house. Sometimes the owner is still home so be sure to communicate with them that you will be in contact immediately after the open house with all offers and feedback. If the owner is not there then just proceed in making sure the house looks in good shape....

- Scan the outside of the house
    - pick up any debris that may have blown into the yard
    - if it has snowed, make sure the pathways are shoveled and the access to the basement if outdoors is also clear of snow and ice.
    - bring in the trash bins if they are on the sidewalk

- Set up signage
    - place your open house sign on the lawn facing the direction of the home and visible to passersby
    - also place a sign out of the main road indicating the direction of the open house with your name and company logo on it
    - place the 3rd and 4th sign at the end of the street where your open house is (one on each end of the street)
- Scan the interior of the house
    - pick any toys that may trip a potential buyer or buyer's agent.
- Lights
    - Turn on all lights as necessary
- Bathrooms

✓   Be sure all toilets are flushed.

✓   **Heat**

     ✓   Make sure the home is a comfortable temperature

✓   **Ambiance**

     ✓   fresh cut flowers or light music to liven up the home

✓   **Sell this!**

     ✓   Set up your marketing materials sign in sheets, business cards, blank offer forms, etc

Inside the home, walk the entire house to be sure it is tidied up (and it should be if you used Marie Kondo's method or used a professional organizer or stagger. If there are any lingering odors, use your air freshener spray (I like the natural citrus spray) or simply try opening the windows. Fluff the pillow, straighten up the bed ...if the carpet is a mess, pull it up if it is an area carpet or vacuum up the dust.

Lights: Turn on all lights as needed. If there is ample sunlight and the room looks better with natural light, then leave the light off in that room. Be sure the entryway and basements are all well-lit as well as the closet spaces. If this is an evening open house, then of course have all the lights on, as well as the landscaping outdoor lights to best show your home.

Lawn signs: should you add balloons or no balloons, that is the question? Personally, I like balloons, but remember I am Switzerland so feel free to decide for yourself if you want to use them. Tying balloons to your open house sign is a great way to help buyers find your open house. I have had several open houses on main roads where buyers were out looking at a different property, saw the balloons for my open house and decided to stop in!

Tie those balloons tightly! You don't want them blowing away and getting caught in the neighbors' trees...NOT FUN!! This happened to me and made my life miserable for a couple of weeks. There were heavy winds during one of my open houses and unbeknownst to me, the balloons got loose. An angry neighbor came storming into the open house demanding I take the balloons down.

I apologized for the inconvenience and processed to look out the window and see the balloons in his tree - 50 feet up! He demanded I get the balloons down immediately, so I asked him if he wanted me to call the fire department? He refused as he thought that would damage his lawn. I figured the wind would blow them down, but this guy was out for me. I ended up having a good conversation with him about the farm, and how his family owned it at one point (maybe this was where the anger was coming from). I asked him if he wanted to own it again, but he didn't go for it.

When I left the balloons were still up there and sure enough, I got a threatening email which I sent along to my manager. The balloons blew down on their own, but it was not fun and a true annoyance for me to deal with for the days that the neighbor was out to ruin this sale.

Balloons on the loose can make for a difficult showing....so tie them down!

Pets

Vacuum up! Nothing is more unappealing to a buyer than walking into a beautiful home and smelling wet dog. Use air freshener if that works. I have seen buyers run out of an open house because the dog odor was so intense their eyes were watering and they were gagging. Please make it easy for someone to buy your house and neutralize odors in the home.

Make sure that you have vacuumed up all the pet hair and that any animal droppings have been properly disposed of. If carpets need to be pulled up, do not hesitate, just do it. Clean and neat is how we want this house. So many people suffer with allergies, so always let potential buyers know there an animal does live there.

Lastly, be sure that animals have been removed from the house during the open house. The liability around this is tremendous, if anything were to happen to a prospective buyer on account of the animal. Have the owners take their pets with them until after the open house.

Dress for success

Always put your best face forward!

Present yourself as a professional. Dress a step up of your target market. If your market is entry level buyers...this is the biggest purchase they have ever made...so present yourself appropriately! What do the staff wear when you visit the Ritz? They are always dressed impeccably and so should you!

I am in New England and last winter was up to my thighs in snow putting lawn sign riders up and walking around in the snow and mud during appraisals; I get it, it's a fine line between being practical and looking your best. So, if you need to boots, wear nice boots with good treads! You can be dressed for the weather and dressed for success!

Real estate is a 24/7 job. You just never know when someone is going to text or call you to look at a property, so if you are not accustomed to dressing well for the day, at least pack a bag of professional clothes in your trunk that you can change in to. It worked for Superman □

Closing a Deal

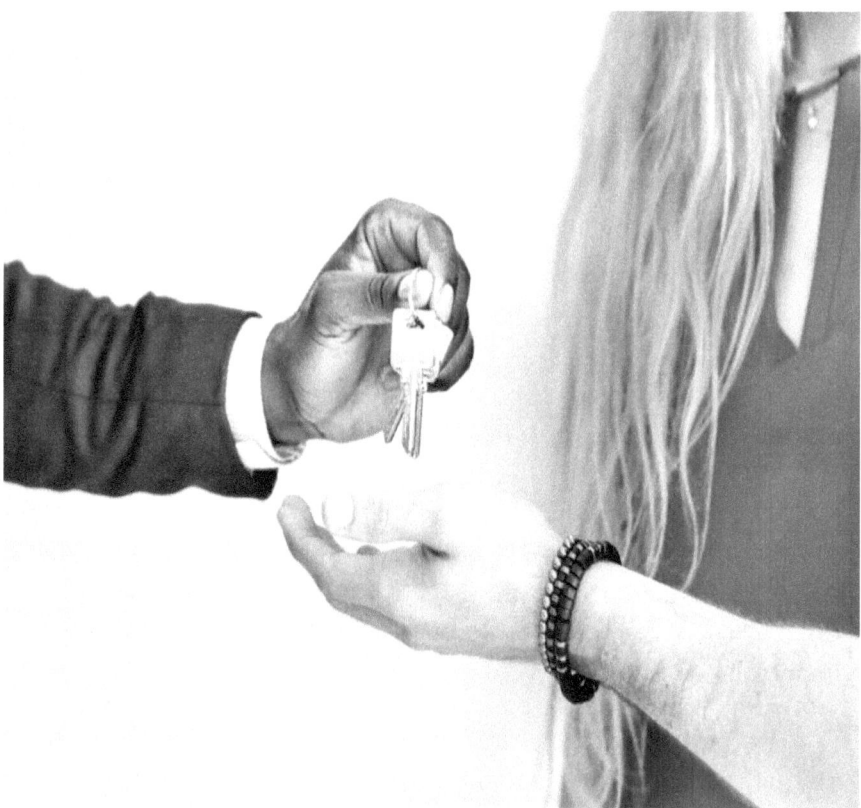

Photo by rawpixel.com from Pexels

Hold on a second, it is NOT over til it's over!

Coming down the home stretch....so you signed your P&S, financing is in place and you are all set to close.... or are You?

Do you have your lawyers lined up?

Have you set the date, time and location of the closing?   Are all parties available to be there in person?   Do they need to have a power of attorney sign for them? Do any documents need to be notarized?

Have you marked your calendar for the closing date?

For all the sellers: make sure all utilities have been notified and any prepayments marked as this will need to be settled during the closing and final payouts made. And for all the buyers make sure you too have notified the utility company that you will be taking over the billing and to keep the utilities turned on!

Be honest

It is so true...honesty is the best policy and as a licensed agent you are legally responsible to relay the truth to your knowledge when asked. If you become a REALTOR®, then you are not only legally but ethically responsible for each transaction you engage in. So just be honest!

What does it mean to be honest?

There are many moving parts to the purchase and sale of a home, but your sole responsibility is to find a willing buyer to transact a real estate sale with. This can be done from the sell side, from producing the seller ...the buy side from bringing in the buyer or by transacting the whole deal by dual agency representing both the buyer and the seller. That is it!

You will be asked "can I build an additional home on the lot?" - if you do not know refer them to the town building department. Do not mislead them with an answer you do not know is true. You will be asked hundreds of questions during each transaction. How old is the roof? Is this septic? Is there water in the basement? If you know the answer to these questions, then you need to relay this information onto the prospective buyers.

There are hundreds of questions you will be asked and be confident in saying, that is out of the scope of what I am hired to do, but I do know that (insert trusted professional here) can help. Honesty is that simple! Not only did you tell the truth but you helped them but pointing them in the right direction - refer them out to your tribe of trusted professionals!

.....and if you don't know the answer....say it.! "I am not sure, but I can find out the exact answer for you and give you a call later today".

So many people have told me that buyers and sellers are both liars ...and while I would love to think that is not true, it often times is the case. It may not be intentional, but it does happen. They just do not want to tell you the whole truth. Often times they want to hide information from you ...because they do not want to have to disclose any flaws in their property and risk a devaluation.

Or from the listing standpoint ...be on top of your business because people are constantly buying and selling their homes...just this weekend, a neighbor mentioned they are selling their main home (and listed with another agent) and a friend is building a house and just sold their (with another agent)...these are tough pills to swallow as a new agent, but with persistence and a good marketing campaign, you will soon enough become top of mind as the trusted real estate agent for all your friends, family, neighbors and the greater community.

Think strategically and objectively

What is the objective of this deal? There are endless reasons why people buy and sell real estate. Your job is to find out as soon as possible in your interactions with them their reason for buying or selling. It is very much like your WHY or PURPOSE for being a real estate agent. Once you have this "why" you can provide them with more tailored listings, and start to speak their language. From there you can find out what their true timeline is so you are sure to deliver accordingly.

☐ Was there a divorce and does that person need a new place to live?

☐ If so why?

Did they land a New job that requires them to move out of

state?

Or closer to the city or their office?

Do they want to be closer to Family?

Or perhaps further away from Family?

What about Price?

Are they paying too much to someone else (rent) right now?

- [ ] What is their Dream?

- [ ] Are they looking to buy their dream house?

- [ ] Or build the house of their dreams?

- [ ] Is this their vacation home?

- [ ] Or place to go on the weekends?

- [ ] Why are they looking or moving?

- [ ] Is this property an investment? Short term? Flip? Long term?

- [ ] Will they be remodeling to flip it (line up your contractor referrals)?

- [ ] Do they intend on holding their investment and renting the property?

- [ ] Are they taking advantage of capital gain tax breaks?

Being equipped with this information will help you to best serve your clients. You will have a thorough understanding of their time frame, what they are looking for in their next property, what they are looking to gain financially from the sale of this property, as well as their expectations of you - their agent!

Know your customers and know your sh*t!

Look at each deal from multiple viewpoints. The more you prepare yourself when going into a deal, the better your chances of getting the results you and your clients are looking for.

What is a win for the buyer?

What is a win for the seller?

What could prevent this deal from moving forward?

What are the obstacles I need to look out for?

Secondly you want to learn as much as you can from the other side of the transaction. This will help you negotiate your deal. Why are they selling? Are they in bankruptcy?

→   Is the house behind in mortgage payments?

→   Is the bank calling in the loan?

→   Has there been catastrophic damage to the home?

→   Is it infested with mold?

Learn as much as you can from the other agent so that you both can work together to get the deal closed.

"Constant kindness can accomplish much.

As the sun makes ice melt,

kindness causes misunderstanding, mistrust, and hostility

to evaporate."

-Albert Schweitzer

Kindness matters

Real estate can be very stressful. There are so many people involved in each transaction and you are in the middle managing it all. Each person has their own ideas and agendas and each person has varying degrees of communication skills. Yes, some people actually think you can read their minds.

Remember to keep a beginner's mind. Do not assume you know what someone means, want or is saying. Ask layers upon layers of questions until you are crystal clear. Now, don't be annoying when you do this, but ask the questions from a standpoint of sincerity and with the intention to help through clear understanding. Notice when someone is not saying what they feel and take the risk to ask them what they want or need.

Everyone wants to feel validated and in multi person transactions like real estate, it is even more important to have it all out on the table so you can work through it. Good, bad or indifferent. Let it be known. Conversely, this is not YOUR deal....so refrain from sharing too much of your personal opinions etc...your job is to get your buyers, sellers, renters to share as much information with you so that you can help them reach their goal and find or sell their real estate.

There are also in person or face to face meetings, but be sure you know your business before meeting a client. Think at least 3 steps ahead! Be sure you look professional, confident and have their best interest in mind. Be a good listener to fully understand how you can best serve their real estate needs.

SO, TAKE A DEEP BREATH and EXHALE before sending that text or email or picking up the phone in anger. Relax and think it through, then make the call or send the text/email.... with KINDNESS. Not everyone is equipped with your knowledge, expertise or experience or skill set. Be kind and patient with everyone you meet. We are all doing our best.

Your Personal Wellness

Put yourself first.

It is a simple as that. Just like on an airplane they tell you to put your oxygen mask on before trying to help others, the same goes in life. Take care of yourself so that you can help others! Be sure you get your rest when you need it ...and guess what naps are indeed ok and healthy for you! Spend some money to get your hair done and nails done if that makes you feel confident and sure of yourself.

Go to the gym, or go for a walk, run or do some gardening. Movement helps keep you balanced and focused.   A body in motion stays in motion. For me nothing gives me more energy and clarity than being out in nature (except when I am in the midst of a great real estate deal)! If the stress gets to be too much, go take a hike, literally get out in the woods and take a step back.

Often times this has led me to have great breakthroughs or ideas that resolve whatever it is that is stressing me out. It is like I have to get out of my own way...and nothing does that better than being in nature...hiking, surfing, walking through the woods, walking the beach, gardening ...a close second to this is going to a library or a museum....

Taking deep breaths throughout the day help bring oxygen to your brain and relieve tension and stress. If you feel your blood starting to boil, talk a few deep breaths, trust that everything will work out fine and go for a walk if you need to. Drop it for a moment, then come back to it when you are calm.

Being a REALTOR® requires nerves of steel. There are highs and lows like no other job and everything is always at stake and on the line. You need to keep your health and wellness a priority to deal with this high level of stress. Take that yoga class, go for a run and meditate! Your body and mind will thank you!

"You can't be that kid

standing at the top of the waterslide,

overthinking it.

You have to go down the chute."

- Tina Fey

Mind frame

Mind frame and belief systems are at the core of your business (and your personal wellness)! It is the thoughts about yourself, the market, your peers and your potential that streams through your mind throughout the day.

Maintaining a positive mind frame is something that can be learned, and mastered with practice. If you are normally a pessimistic person, it will take a huge leap of faith to move you over to the positive side, but you can do it!

In sales they say: "fake it til you make it" and that is the same with creating a positive frame of mind.

This is that subtle voice that either knocks you down and tells you to throw in the towel, or it is that voice of hope and optimism that tells you to take a deep breath, pick up the phone and make that call you are dreading making. Rip that Band-Aid off and just do it. When you have doubts or are experiencing high stress, take a deep breath. Step away from the issue for a moment and allow some space for an enlightened answer to come to mind. Try it!

For more support, you can read positive psychology books by my favorites: Tony Robbins, Wayne Dyer, Deepak Chopra, Eckhart Tolle or Louise Hay. Or you can log into you tube and look up "positive affirmations" and listen to recording of positive and encouraging words.

This may be out of your comfort zone, but lean into it and give it a whirl!

"Everything

you have ever

Wanted

Is on

The other side

of fear"

-   George Addir

Richard Branson, founder of the Virgin Empire notes "as someone who's pushed my own expectations time and time again, and put myself in risky situations over and over, I couldn't agree more. We all feel fear at some point in life, particularly when starting out at something new. Fear is a healthy human emotion, so long as it doesn't cripple other emotions to get in the way of opportunity."

This is a 100% commission business (unless you are a RedFin agent or have some special deal with your broker). That means you do not get a regular paycheck. This can be very challenging and it is so important to keep your mind clear of worry and concern and to focus on the positive outcome you are aiming for – a successful career as a REALTOR®.

Branson continues: *"The moral of the story: Don't let fear hold you back from achieving your full potential. Harness it and channel it into passion. Everything you've ever wanted is on the other side of fear.*

Setting the stage each day with a positive optimistic mind frame is essential to living a happy, healthy and thriving life. You may not always feel like it; but trust me on a subconscious level the more you remind yourself of how great you are and how amazing your career is, it will begin to happen. Fake it until you make it. Morning mantras or affirmations are an easy way to get your head on straight and start your day off right.

Some of my favorite people I refer to when starting off and selecting my mantras include: Louise Hay, Tony Robbins and Wayne Dyer.

✓ Today is a wonderful day of prosperity.

✓ My business is booming!

✓ I treat each person I encounter with total love and respect.

✓ My sales grow each day.

✓ My clients love me and refer me to their network.

✓ I am happy, healthy and successful.

✓ Better and better every day in every way.

Some people find reciting these words in front of a mirror help amplify their results. So, you may want to try that out.

The important thing here is to feel good when you are reciting your affirmations.

It is that positive vibe you are going for. If you are not feeling good, just try for a better feeling. You are looking for relief here. Be easy on yourself and trust that everything will be fine.

These affirmations should be repeated throughout the day. If you feel yourself getting down, just remember to go back to your affirmations and remind yourself of how awesome and successful you are!

→ I AM LIMITLESS

→ I CREATE MY REALITY

→ I CLOSE DEAL OFTEN & WITH EASE

→ I STAND IN MY POWER

→ I CHOOSE TO WORK WITH GREAT PEOPLE

→ I AM FIERCE

→ I LEARN AND MOVE ON FROM MY MISTAKES

→ EVERYTHING IS POSSIBLE

→ THE RESOURCES I NEED ARE ALWAYS THERE FOR ME

→ I AM LOVED

→ I AM CONFIDENT

→ I AM INTELLIGENT

→ I AM HAPPY

→ I AM FLEXIBLE

→ MY ENERGY IS ENDLESS

→ I AM SOLUTION DRIVEN

→ MY WORK FULFILLS ME

→ OBSTACLES ARE FUN AND CHALLENGE ME TO GROW AND THINK IN NEW WAYS

→ I AM OPEN TO NEW IDEAS

→ I AM CREATIVE

→ I ACT WITH PERFECT & COMPLETE INTENT

→ I AM GRATEFUL

→ MY LIFE IS MY MASTERPIECE

→ I AM MINDFUL

→ I AM CALM AND CONFIDENT

→ I LOVE MYSELF AND OTHERS

→ I ATTRACT POSITIVE PEOPLE AND LOVE

→ I GIVE LIFE MY BEST AND LIFE GIVES ME THE BEST!

Write down some of your own favorite affirmations, or make some up that resonate with you!

_____

_____

_____

_____

_____

_____

_____

_____

Continute writing some of your favorite affirmations:

_____

_____

_____

_____

_____

_____

_____

_____

AND IT IS SO!

"Formal education

will make you a living;

self-education

will make you a fortune."

-Jim Rohn

Always continue to learn

Life is a classroom. It really is! Most people think learning mainly happens in school...but what about what happens in the schoolyard and after school? That's where life happens.

Maybe you didn't like school per say, and that is ok. The structure and rigidity is certainly not for everyone; but we are all in this huge classroom called life together. We learn new things each and every day by experience and interaction with our surroundings and others; by things that happen to us, events that we participate in or happen in the larger world around us. Whether we realize it or not we are learning creatures who continue to explore, learn and grow.

Take charge of your learning. I drive a lot and have learned so many amazing skills and subjects by listening to books on tape, podcasts or from audible.com. Many of the classics are available for free or maybe you want to sign up for Audible. To be honest I am an avid reader, but lately with apps on my smartphone, I have noticed my attention span is about 3 seconds at this point. For some reason it is more of a challenge for me to focus in on a book with my eyes, than it is to listen with me ears...so listen it is! If you are old school or on a budget, many libraries have books on CD you can borrow too.

It is much cheaper to learn beforehand, than learn the lesson afterwards.....

Learning prepares us for the world. It gives us examples of what is out there and tools we can try to improve our lives and livelihoods. Give it a go! Make learning part of your daily routine. A chapter a day is all it takes ...then add on. The quiet time of book reading is also a nice break from the world of sensory overload we live in.

"Here's to the crazy ones.

The misfits. The rebels.

The troublemakers.

The round pegs in the square holes.

The ones who see things differently.

They're not fond of rules.

And they have no respect for the status quo.

You can quote them, disagree with them, glorify or vilify them.

About the only thing you can't do is ignore them.

Because they change things.

They push the human race forward.

And while some may see them as the crazy ones,

we see genius.

Because the people who are crazy enough to think

they can change the world,

are the ones who do."

-Steve Jobs

Acknowledgments

Susan A. Gillis

Wayne Dyer

Babson College

AMMA

Tony Robbins

Jack Childs

Steve Jobs

Deepak Chopra

Linda A. Mason

Donna Fitzgerald

ST JOHN

Gina Brennan

Carol Hewett

Bloomingdale's

Katie Blaeser

Abbott

Jason Goldner

Marie Kondo

Vernon Coffey

Erin Sheehan

Thomas P. Gillis

Edward & Mary Canniff

Jenna M. Reedy

Emily Tighe

Deb Bruckner

His Holiness the Dalai Lama

Melissa Lind

Bruce Whittredge

Dougal & Mary Gillis

Lisa Davenport

Brent Tartamella

Abraham Hicks

Maximilian

Louise Hay

Guy Kawasaki

Corporate Visions

Coldwell Banker

Coldwell Banker

Eric Robinson

Thomas M. & Kerri K. Gillis

Nancy Gordon

Jack Conway RE

Abby Grundler

ADP

Catherine Ponder

Salve Regina University

Ann O'Neil

Roderick

Boston Latin School

Eddie Canniff

Melanie Brewster

The Junior League of Boston

It is with gratitude that I thank each one here. You are my teachers, my mentors, my guides, my managers, my family and my friends. Half of you I have worked with directly, the other half through your teachings. I am deeply grateful for the ways you have molded me, shaped me and believed in me. It is my desire to share these gifts with others.

Dear Readers,

Congratulations on embarking on this exciting career as a real estate agent or REALTOR®! You have your work cut out for you, but I trust you will hit the ground running towards your success.

Little by little each day, you will become more knowledgeable, more confident and more capable of making all of your dreams a reality. Use your resources, trust your instincts and keep giving it your best!

Remember to check in with me, I want to hear how you are building your dream life and exceeding your goals!

Jump on my facebook page any chance you get : https://www.facebook.com/susiegillisREALTOR/ or send me a message through my website www.SusieGillis.com and let me know how RYRY is working out for you! There are no limits in this field. NONE. Your income is unstoppable and your ability to help people find the homes of their dreams is limitless. The possibilities are endless and the canvas is blank for you to create the masterpiece of your life.

Seize the day and always work with love,

SKG

Susan K. Gillis, M.A.

About the Author

Susan K. Gillis "Susie" was born and raised in Boston, MA. She is a licensed REALTOR® in the state of MA and has spent the last 20 years working in both corporate and small business sales and consulting; launching, building and helping to build holistic infrastructures while maximizing productivity and the bottom line through technology and people.

Her mission statement in 2003 remains the same today: *"to let the world know they can make a living doing what they love"*.

Susie graduated from Boston Latin School, holds her Bachelor's degree from Babson College in Entrepreneurial Studies and continues to mentor through Babson's Coaching for Leadership Program. She holds her Master's degree in Holistic Leadership from Salve Regina University and has furthered her Master's studies with work in Alternative Health and Healing with the Learning Institute (learn.edu). She is a Reiki Master Teacher, RYT 200 with Frog Lotus Yoga, Silva Method Graduate and adoring aunt to the most incredible girls.

In addition to selling real estate, you can find Susie substitute teaching on all grade levels in Marshfield & Duxbury, MA school systems, volunteering, consulting, travelling, writing and being present with the joys and flow of life.

Susie lives on the South Shore of Massachusetts.

Age quod agis!

www.ingramcontent.com/pod-product-compliance
Lightning Source LLC
Chambersburg PA
CBHW021352210526
45463CB00001B/75